A Treasury of Sussex Folklore

Tony Wales

S.B. Publications

**To the memory of Lillian Candlin who opened
so many Sussex windows for me**

First published in 2000 by S B Publications
19 Grove Road, Seaford, Sussex BN25 1TP
01323 893498
fax 01323 893860
sales@sbpublications.swinternet.co.uk

ISBN 1 85770 217 4

Front cover painting by Mick Bensley

Typeset by JEM Editorial, Lewes (JEMedit@AOL.com)

Printed by Tansleys the Printers
19 Broad Street
Seaford
East Sussex BN25 1LS
01323 891019

INTRODUCTION

If this book needed an additional title it might be *Folklore Can Be Fun.* This would not imply that the material was lightweight, or of little importance, but merely that the book is written to entertain rather than instruct. There are, of course, many fine works dealing with folklore on an academic level, but this book is not intended for the expert or the high-powered scholar, but for those who find the quirkiness of the Sussex character infinitely fascinating.

What constitutes folklore? Of course subjects like traditional customs, witchcraft, legends, folk songs and superstitions are bound to be included. But what about country cures, old games, childrens rhymes and weather signs? Well yes, probably all these qualify. But then we are left with things like bull baiting, wife selling, toasts and epitaphs – not forgetting hermits and eccentrics. My self-imposed brief has been to write about some of the obvious subjects, but also to include a fair number of less obvious ones. Which opens up the question of where does folklore and social history part company. I leave you the reader to decide.

I am sometimes asked how I first became interested in all this 'old stuff' connected with Sussex. Very difficult to be certain, but I feel sure my mother had something to do with it. She came from a family where ancient beliefs, home-made cures and dialect words were part of everyday life. She saw no reason to apologise for this, even if so often she appeared out of step with the present century. So I feel certain that a lot of her family wisdom rubbed off on to me as a child. Subsequently writers like Arthur Beckett sparked my interest in all things Sussex, and later it was author Lillian Candlin who really set my feet on the road to the discovery of Sussex folklore.

After a reasonably long life, lived always in West Sussex, I have been very fortunate in meeting so many older Sussex folk who have been willing to share the riches of their own lives with me. My notebooks and tapes are bulging with their memories, and I am eternally grateful for being allowed to share in so much of this inherited wisdom.

*St Dunstan's relics at Mayfield
– see under Devil*

In this present book you will find a lot has been left out – the original draft was about three times the present length, and even that was only a fraction of what could have been included. You will also find tales and beliefs different from similar ones already known to you. This is the great fascination of folklore, in that so much that is essentially the same, still differs greatly from one locality, or one family, to another. If you know different versions from the ones I have used, then please do not conclude that I have got it wrong – but send me a note letting me have your particular version. I have now written more than twenty books, large and small, on Sussex subjects, and every one has added to my knowledge, because so many kind readers have written to me afterwards with additional information. And of course it all goes into those bulging notebooks.

Thank you for buying this book, and happy reading.

Tony Wales
Horsham 2000

ALFRISTON CHURCH

THE glorious Church of St Andrew, Alfriston, known affectionately as the Cathedral of the Downs, was built about 1360. It stands on a mound, part of the village green, called here the Tye.

Legend says that it was the villagers' intention to build their church on a piece of land known as Sayne Croft to the west of the Tye. When the work was started, the stones placed ready for use the next day were, each night, removed by a supernatural force, and were found on the Tye. After several attempts to build in the original place, the workmen gave up and erected the church where it now stands. This story is similar to others which exist all over Sussex (and elsewhere, including Durham Cathedral), and may be explained by the conflict which existed between those who wished to build the new church on an old pagan site,and others who resisted the new religion.

In this particular version of the story there is an additional twist, when it was noticed by a 'wise man' that four oxen were lying together with their rumps touching, thus forming a cross – so this was taken as a divine sign that a cruciform church should be erected on that very spot. A slightly different version of the story involves St Anthony, who wished to build a church near the coast in Sussex. He landed at Cuckmere Haven, walked up the valley and arrived at a field where he lay down to rest. Here he dreamed of the sight of four oxen lying rump to rump, and so we are back at the same ending.

Church of St Andrew, Alfriston

ALFRISTON CROSS

THE battered Market Cross in Waterloo Square (known to locals as The Square) is one of only two in the county, the other being the rather grander example in Chichester. It was once used regularly for local announcements and was a focus for the market and many other local events. Originally it was more imposing, with four stone steps. In 1833 it was partly demolished and the stone of the steps was taken away and used to make drains and doorsteps etc. At this time it was topped with a hat-like stone, supposed to represent a shepherd's crown fossil, as found on the Downs. A drawing from 1787 shows the cross much taller than at present, but by 1835 it had become almost a completely new edifice, with modern bricks and stonework added. Since then it has been damaged by traffic several times.

The cross was probably first erected in the fifteenth century to become the centrepiece of the weekly market (there were once also two annual fairs on April 30 and November 29). In 1837 it was joined by a chestnut tree, although the present tree is not the original.

Alfriston Market Cross, a rarity in Sussex

ALL SAINTS' CHURCH, ROFFEY

THIS is a fine local story, which has been described as 'The Legend of Roffey'.

The church in this village north of Horsham was built by Gertrude Martyn in memory of her late husband, Captain Cecil Edward Martyn, who died in 1870 at the early age of thirty-three. Built of stone from the fabled St Leonard's Forest (*ibid*), it was consecrated by the Bishop of Chichester on All Saints Day, 1878.

On a fine November morning, the workmen were putting the finishing touches to the building when, suddenly, a large white bird flew towards it, dashing itself against the wooden scaffolding, and falling dead at the base of the church tower. It was a wild white swan, and its lovely plumage was preserved and became the original decoration of the front of the main altar. When the feathers started to disintegrate, the remainder were used on a canopy for processions. The Martyn family crest was a white swan rising out of a crown, and Mrs Martyn felt the incident was a good omen for the life of the new church.

A poem written in 1886 by Richard Wilton, tells the story:

> The darkling dawn had come of All Saints' Day;
> The votive church awaits the solemn hour
> Of dedication. The consummate flower
> Of Pious love sighs for the sun's first ray.
> Then flashed a sign athwart the twilight grey
> To sooth the mourner with a mystic power:
> A swan in its swift flight, struck the Church tower
> And at its base, in lifeless beauty, lay.
> The wondering Foundress welcomed the dear Crest,
> Pledge of her loved one's sympathy that morn;
> And now the fair white plumes from wing and breast
> The altar's frontal on festal days adorn.
> Stamped with the Cross and Crown, that tell of rest
> For all Christ's saints beyond this life forlorn!

ANNE OF CLEVES HOUSE, LEWES

THIS is one of two Sussex buildings connected with Anne of Cleves, the other being in Ditchling. Although bearing her name, it is doubtful if King Henry's divorced Queen ever lived in either. Now this building is owned by the Sussex Archaeological Society, and functions as a local museum.The porch bears the date 1599, although it is thought that some portions of the house may be older. The building was presented to the society in 1925 by the late Frank Verrrall, Lord of the Manor of Southover.

From the folklore aspect, there are vague stories of the house being haunted, and being avoided by locals at some period in its history. More interesting is the large octagonal table, with a Sussex marble top, which once was used by the monks at Malling Monastery, near Lewes. The legend attached to this is that on a stormy night in 1170, the murderers of

Anne of Cleves House

Thomas a Becket, having fled west from Canterbury, deposited their arms on the table while they sat warming themselves at the fire and discussing the dreadful deed they had committed. The table then began to shake and all the weapons fell to the floor. They were replaced, but again the table shook them off.

Unfortunately, like many other equally interesting stories, the date given to the table by experts conflicts with the period of the legend.

ASCENSION DAY

ONCE known as Holy Thursday, this is forty days after Easter – always referred to when I was at school as 'The Great Forty Days', in other words the days when Jesus remained on earth after his resurrection, prior to his ascension into Heaven. The day is central to the church season of Rogationtide (a time of prayer, particularly for the year's harvest), which includes the Monday, Tuesday and Wednesday before Ascension Day itself. The preceding Sunday was known as Rogation Sunday.

In many counties the day is dedicated to water and wells (for instance the well known well dressings in Derbyshire). Customs of this sort must reach back to well before Christianity. In Sussex the church has been more involved with the observance of Rogation walks, which have merged into beating of the bounds in several places.

There are a few local customs worthy of notice. In Slinfold in the 1940s, most of the school children wore sprays of lily of the valley to symbolise 'a ladder up to Heaven'. In East Grinstead in the same period, the market was blessed early in the morning by the vicar, with his attendant choir boys – a custom evidently connected with the Rogationtide processions. At Plumpton Green, Raymond Woods (quoted by Rupert Taylor in his *East Sussex Village Book*) recalled schooldays in the village when it was a local tradition on Ascension Day for the children to walk two miles to a service at St Michael's Church, Plumpton, then climb to the Cross on the Downs (*ibid*). Here they enjoyed a sandwich lunch, and afterwards gave vent to their high spirits by sliding on their bottoms down the hill below Black Cap.

ASH WEDNESDAY

Young marble players in Rye

AFTER the activities of Shrove Tuesday, Ash Wednesday was comparatively quiet in Sussex. In some places it was known as Pinching Day – a title usually reserved for Oak Apple Day (May 29). Children were expected to take ash twigs to school, with the ends blackened with ink or mud. No trace of white should be in evidence, not even a white hanky. Failure to observe this custom would result in the culprit being pinched, or otherwise chastised by the other children, although all this had to cease at noon. This happened in schools in Cowfold, Crowborough, Forest Row, Henfield, Hurstpierpoint, Plumpton, Lewes, Sayers Common and Selmeston (and no doubt in other places as well). There were a number of local variations.

Ash Wednesday was perhaps better known as the first day of the marble season, which climaxed on Good Friday, both for adults and children. Other games which began on this day included skipping and bat and trap, both of which also reached their greatest popularity on Good Friday (*ibid*).

BARREL ORGANS IN SUSSEX CHURCHES

SOMETIMES known as winch organs, or more romantically as seraphims, these little organs enjoyed a brief period of popularity in village churches. They appear here as, apart from the primitive quality of the sound, they also attracted a number of good stories, and it was obvious that everything about the instruments appealed to the Sussex countryman's sense of humour.

Most had ten or twelve barrels, each pricked with individual tunes, and these could be secular as well as sacred. Sometimes the operator, who was usually the parish clerk, would have to wind through several unwanted tunes.

Jevington (where the rhyme said that 'Jevington poor people, sold their bells to repair their steeple') had the reputation of being the most musical village in the area. When parishioners decided to have a barrel organ in their church, it was brought from London in a wagon. A farmer's wife ordered an early type of washing machine at the same time, and by mistake the organ was left at the farm and the washing machine delivered to the church. Apparently the mistake was discovered before too much harm was done. But their troubles did not end there. The organ was supposed to play only one tune (*The Old Hundredth*), but one Sunday after this it went on to the lively air *Little Drops of Brandy*. All attempts to bring this to an end failed, so the vicar grabbed it in his arms and threw it down the village well – or as some versions of the tale have it, it was dumped in the churchyard to play itself out. Afterwards ghostly wails were said to emanate from the well, and it was felt that the ghost of the organ was still complaining.

Strong doubts as to the genuineness of these accounts is aroused by the same stories being attached to other Sussex villages, such as Berwick.

The barrel organ in Piddinghoe was said to have been used in the village inn on weekdays and then moved to the church on Sundays. Obviously the thought of any instrument that could play dance tunes as well as sacred melodies was too much for the village tale tellers, and many good stories must have resulted, although not recorded for posterity.

BEATING THE BOUNDS

TRADITIONALLY the ceremony of beating the bounds of the parish was carried out at Rogation time. It was essentially a church-inspired custom, and was intended to familiarise the villagers, and especially the younger folk, with the boundaries of the place where they lived. Willow wands were used to beat the ground. The children taking part might also be beaten or bumped, to impress the lesson more forcibly upon them – although we assume this would have been more in fun than in earnest. A typical event would include prayers by the vicar, with a cross being made upon the ground at certain points, and frequent stops for refreshments. Sometimes only a small number turned out, or the event might be well supported with plenty of food and drink provided.

Although usually considered annual events, often the boundary beatings were allowed to lapse for a few years, until some public spirited villager whipped up enough enthusiasm to get the whole thing going once again.

Some idea of the food and drink consumed at these community perambulations can be gleaned by looking at Burpham in 1705,

The clergy, the schoolmaster, the town fathers and a schoolgirl are pictured beating of the bounds at Hastings in 1926

12

when eight to ten gallons of ale, a two-gallon loaf of bread, a two-gallon cake, and cheese were consumed. Again in 1711 the shopping list included six gallons of ale, a gallon loaf of bread, cakes and cheese. By 1810 the food and drink provided had increased to include twenty-three gallons of ale, several gallons of bread and cakes, and an unknown quantity of cheese. How many people took part is not known, but Burpham is not a huge place, so they were not expected to walk on an empty stomach.

A great many Sussex parishes have records of their boundary ceremonies in the past, but I can only mention a few. At Bexhill the parish boundary was marked in 1902 by sixty-three large stones. The beating of these stones took place in 1905, 1925 and 1928, when some of the town councillors were ceremoniously bumped. In 1952 attempts were made to trace the stones, but these failed.

In 1777 the inhabitants of Washington and Findon joined together to beat their bounds, with the vicar, two gentlemen, a labourer and two youths. No doubt this was considered a good cross section of the population at that time.

On the border of West Sussex with Hampshire, at the Flying Bull Inn, Rake, boys were put into the bread oven to remind them of the boundary which was said to run through the bar.

Sometimes disputes arose over the boundaries. This happened at Northiam in the nineteenth century, when maps were drawn up and signed by the rector and others concerned. On May 4, 1826, the boundaries between Beckley and Northiam were ceremoniously walked by the rector, churchwardens and their congregation.

In modern times beating the bounds may not be so necessary, but it is still carried out with enthusiasm at a number of places, including the county town, Lewes, and larger towns such as Hastings and Littlehampton.

BEES

BEES are unique in many respects, and they exert a definite fascination over quite a lot of people. Part of this is tied up to the many old customs and superstitions which surround them. Most older beekeepers will tell you that it is important to talk to bees, and this is particularly so where marriages and funerals are taking place in the family. If the bees are not informed of a death, then they will almost certainly leave the hive, and another death will surely follow. The custom is to place a strip of black material around the hive, and to tap with a door key on the side, telling them exactly what has taken place.

For a birth, a piece of white material can be used, and if this is not done then the child will find honey repugnant. At a wedding the bees should always be provided with a piece of wedding cake. When visiting a bee-keeper for the first time, be sure to agree to the request to 'come and meet the bees'.

Other bee superstitions included the belief that if the bees make a nest on the roof of the house, then none of the daughters would marry. Even more unpleasant was the idea that a swarm on a hedge-stack would mean an imminent death. Bees like to be included in the Christmas festivities, so you should allow them a dinner in the form of a block of candy for each hive. A nice Christmas belief was that if you put your ear to the hive at midnight on Christmas Eve then you will hear the bees humming a carol.

Bees must always be informed of the change of ownership of the hive, or they will keep on swarming. Ideally bees should not be sold, but exchanged. If money has to be used, then it must be gold.

A rhyme once common in Sussex went like this:

A swarm of bees in May, be worth a load of hay.
A swarm of bees in June, be worth a silver spoon.
But a swarm of bees in July, are not worth a flea.

The old custom of Ringing the Bees – beating a cooking pan when the bees decide to swarm, was very common, and this strange custom has a long and persistent history. The intention seems to be to stake a claim to the bees if they move on to someone else's land.

The ownership of bees was considered very desirable. In 1822 two hives were stolen at Keymer. The owner advertised in the *Lewes Journal* for their return, offering a reward of two guineas over and above what would be given by the Ditchling Prosecuting Society on a conviction.

Wassailing the Bees is a custom less common than the similar one carried out in orchards at the new year. Little is known about this kind of wassailing, but a song collected by the Reverend John Broadwood of Lyne, Rusper has the line 'We'll wassail bees and apple trees', so probably the same gang of men and boys who gathered around the fruit trees on Boxing Day, (or Old Christmas Day), would have carried on to the bee hives for similar junketings. A rhyme said to have been used,went as follows:

> *Bees, o Bees of Paradise, does the work of Jesus Christ.*
> *Does the work which no man can.*
> *God made bees, and bees made honey,*
> *God made man, and man made money,*
> *God made great men to plough and to sow,*
> *God made little boys to tend the rooks and crows,*
> *God made women to brew and to bake,*
> *And God made little girls to eat up all the cake.*
> *Then blow the horn.*

The little boys with the rooks and crows were evidently the bird scarers, and as regards the line about women, I can only plead that this was noted around 1900, when it was certainly very much a 'man's world'.

When I talked about wassailing the bees, during a lecture, a woman beekeeper said that modern imported bees would not take kindly to being disturbed by noisy men and boys around New Year. But she thought that the native English bees, which were more docile, would have been prepared to accept it.

BEGGARS AND TRAMPS

THE folklore of the men of the roads is filled with strange names, and even stranger words. They were known as travellers, wanderers, goer-abouts and roaders, but most often just beggars. A hut where they rested near Exceat was known locally as Beggars Barn. Most villagers exercised their collective minds as to how they could rid themselves of what was seen as a great nuisance. The ideal solution was to persuade the old fellow who was causing the problem to move on to the next parish.

A Loxwood policeman solved the problem by putting drunken tramps in a wheelbarrow and tipping them over the border into the next county – Surrey. But of course this could only be done if you lived in a border village.

The *Lewes and East Sussex Church Magazine* of January 1870 published a plan to rid the neighbourhood of 'imposters'. 'When as is often stated, the beggar is on the point of starvation, he will be supplied with a piece of bread to be eaten under the eye of the Officer.' (At this time it was proposed to establish a Mendicity Society at Lewes.)

On gateposts, the tramps chalked strange signs which they claimed gave warning to fellow travellers of the house occupier's character. Often whole families, with all their possessions in old prams or carts, trundled the roads between workhouses, making regular calls at houses which they knew would provide a welcome. Henry Burstow in his *Reminiscences of Horsham* (1911) wrote of the beggar-pookers, who were expected to assist unwanted beggars out of the parish. For this they were provided with a pole about 6ft long, and nearly as thick as the wrist. If the gentlemen concerned would not move at the desired pace, they would find the pole pressing into the small of their backs. Obviously beggar-pooking was not an easy job. One day a beggar in Guildford accosted Burstow's brother asking him, 'Is old Potter, the beggar-pooker still alive?' When told that he had died, the beggar replied, 'Then I can go to Horsham again; the last time I was there that old .... pooked me all the way down the Bishopric out of the town, but when we got to the bottom I up with my fist and knocked him head-over-heels. I bolted off then, and have never been there since'.

Burstow also described an important wedding in Horsham, in

1837, that of the Queen of the Beggars otherwise known as Mrs Simpson, who kept a common lodging house known as The Beggars' Opera in Brighton Road. Her bridegroom was John Cole, known as King Cole or King of the Rooks – the latter title arising from the fact that he lived in The Rookery (the usual name for The Bishopric). The townsfolk were said to be much relieved when this wedding had taken place, as previously the Queen, who was somewhat fickle, had betrothed herself to a tramp, and on the appointed day had a stand-up fight with him.

Most country people were too poor themselves to have much to spare for their travelling brethren. Patcham churchwardens' accounts in 1705 stated: 'Wayfaring men passing through receive one penny' (at that time a typical full day's wage).

Blind Harry, a Brighton street musician, c1900s

BELLS

It was the Sussex author Arthur Beckett who pointed out that Sussex is a county of bells – church bells, sheep bells and carter's bells. Many of the references to bells in Sussex folklore are in rhyme:

Six are the bells of Fittleworth.
Some like them well,
But sad to tell,
Some say they are but little-worth.

Then there is a whole litany of bell rhymes:

Business finished, work begin, says the bells of Alfriston.
An old woman limping, says the bells of Clymping.
I'll give you a slap on the pate, says the bells of Eastergate.
Bread and cheese on a board, says the bells of Ford.
Come in and welcome, says the bells of Felpham.
Hurry up or you'll be late, says the bells of Faygate.
There's more rogues than honest men, says the bells of
  Warbleton.
Shut the gate and clap'n, says the bells of Yapton.

All Saints church at Hastings, has its Belfry Rules in rhyme:

This is a belfry that is free,
For all those that civil be.
And if you please to chime or ring,
It is a very pleasant thing.

There is no musick played or sung,
Like unto bells when they're well rung.
Then ring your bells well if you can,
Silence is best for every man.

But if you ring in spur or hat,.
Sixpence you pay be sure of that.
And if a bell you overthrow,
Please pay a groat before you go.

Elsewhere the ringers were advised thus:

Ye ringers all who prize,
Your health and happiness.
Be sober, merry, wise.
And you'll the same possess.

Many interesting inscriptions appear on the bells themselves, and here are a few examples:

To honour both of God and King, our voices shall in concert
ring.

Whilst thus we join in joyful sound, may love and loyalty
abound.

Ye people all who hear me ring, be faithful to your God and
King.

Our voices shall with joyful sound, make hills and valleys echo
round

Although I am both light and small, I will be heard above you
all.

I mean to make it understood,that though I'm little, yet I'm
good.

Founders and donors were not forgotten, as in this rhyme:

This is to show to ages yet to come,
That by subscription we were cast and hung.
And Edward Lilham is the name,
That was the actor of the same.

There are many bell legends telling of how the church bells became lost in a pool or river, and could be recovered only by magical means. For example, the original bells of Arlington Church were said to lie at the bottom of a deep pool, which became known as Bell

Hole. It was said that they could be rescued only with six pairs of white oxen. Attempts to achieve this were always unsuccessful, when it was discovered at the last moment that one of the beasts had a single white hair.

One of the most often quoted Sussex bell legends concerns the Nowhurst (or as sometimes given, the Rudgwick) bell. This was a huge bell cast in Rome and intended for York Minster. On its way it fell into a bog at Nowhurst Farm, and remained buried there for centuries. In the days of witches, one said that it could be retrieved if a certain number of pure white heifers were used, with a long chain fixed to the bell – but with a proviso that no-one must speak while the deed was being done. When the bell was almost up, a man could contain himself no longer and exclaimed, 'We have done it. We have got the Nowhurst bell'. It sank again instantly. This is a story still told in the vicinity, and there are a great many variants.

Stories of sunken bells abound in Sussex, such as the bells of a monastery which can be heard at times on Shoreham beach. Another extremely well known sunken bell legend relates to Bosham (see the entry under this village).

Many Sussex villages have inns which commemorate their church bells, for instance Five Bells (Chailey), Six Bells (Chiddingly) and Eight Bells (Bolney). Billingshurst also has an inn named Ye Olde Six Bells, although the church actually has had eight since 1892.

Bells on Sussex sheep have been well written about, and Arthur Beckett mentioned the carter's teams. But Ralph Hollingdale told me in 1994 about Major Lane's cows at Ditchling which all wore bells on thick leather straps about their necks. One of an oblong shape had a particularly lovely low tone.

There are some lovely Sussex stories which concern bells. Here are just two examples:

At one bellringers' practice night at Slaugham, beer had been imbibed rather freely. The merry ringers started home around midnight and one of the men getting over a style found himself astride a donkey on the other side. He cried out in fright, 'Oh Good De'il, done take me, I am a good bellringer, not a wicked man'. The donkey, frightened by this outburst, galloped off until the man eventually fell off.

Another good story comes from Burwash, where the bellringers refused to ring their bells when George IV (when Prince of Wales) passed through their village on his way back to Brighton, from a visit to Sir John Lade at Etchingham. The reason given was because when they had rung the bells on the Prince's journey to Sir John, no message had been left concerning the customary free beer. It was unusual for the Prince to overlook something connected with food or drink.

New bell for All Saints Church, Hastings, 1922

BENEFIT CLUBS

NOT all the activities within the village inn were concerned with drinking or fun and games. Some had a very serious side, such as the meetings of the local benefit clubs. The history of these goes back several centuries, although they seem to have been particularly active during the nineteenth and early twentieth centuries. These were a sincere attempt to tackle the problems of sickness and death, before such things were noticed by the state. The annual meetings of the club on what were known as Club Days, were often big affairs locally, with a church parade, and a feast at the pub to round off the day. The men in their Sunday best, which often meant white smocks, would assemble at their pub headquarters and process to the church for a service. Often the men carried staves (said to have been inspired by the Canterbury Pilgrims) and would be led by the village band.

Sometimes the feast that followed became rather more important than the serious side of the club's activities. It was said that certain clubs got into trouble, when the money contributed to alleviate sickness, was frittered away on food and drink for these annual events. Some villages had more than one club, each based on a particular pub. Even workers on a large estate (such as Petworth) had their own Club Day.

Harting in 1912

Members of Harting Club, pictured on Club Day, c1950s

The importance of these annual get-togethers may be judged by one little girl's reply when asked what were the chief festivals of the church. She replied: 'Christmas, Easter and Club Day'.

A Mr Barton, who lived at Rushlake Green, recalled the village club of his youth. They processed to the church every May, carrying peeled staves. A man who became drunk on Club Day was fined two and sixpence (a very large amount at that time). One man was determined to enjoy himself come-what-may, and placed his half-a-crown in front of him at the feast, before he started drinking.

One of the best known Sussex clubs is Harting Old Club, founded early in the nineteenth century, and still going. Another well known club was the Barnes Green Friendly Society, although this had to be disbanded after an existence of more than a century. In its hey-day the club held a service in Itchingfield Church, and after coffee in the Rectory, marched to Muntham House for lunch in a big marquee. The night before, the pub held a Cherry Fair and following the club procession, there was a village fair.

The oldest of the Sussex clubs was probably the Chailey Friendly Society, which began in 1782. The society's motto was 'Love the Brotherhood, Fear God, Honour the King'.

BENDING-IN

SOUTH coast fishermen have always been great custodians of old customs. A very enduring one was known as Bending-In (also known as Bren-cheese and Beer Day), and until the very late nineteenth century was observed in Brighton, Shoreham and Newhaven.

The custom consisted of a meal of bread and cheese, or bread and treacle, provided by the fishermen at the commencement of the mackerel fishing season in late April or early May. The children were not forgotten, with ginger-pop, and even entertainment by the local Punch and Judy man.

The usual explanation for the origin of the tradition was that it was a debased form of Benediction, (a service of adoration and blessing), in pre-reformation times carried out by the priest. Or it could have originated even earlier, when in pagan times food would have been cast into the sea to placate the gods. In more modern times the ceremonies would still have been attended by the local clergyman, who might even be expected to donate to the eatables.

Brighton fishermen landing a catch of mackerel, early 1900s

After the feasting, the fishermen cast their nets, and with their heads bare recited the following:

> *There they goes, then; God Almighty,*
> *Send us a blessing, it is to be hoped.*

As the procedure continued they intoned:

> *Watch barrel, watch. mackerel for to catch.*
> *White may they be, like a blossom on a tree.*
> *God send thousands, one,two.,three.*
> *Some by their heads, some by their tails.*
> *God send thousands, and never fails.*

Meanwhile the women crossed themselves, bowing three times. When the last net was overboard, the master said 'Seas All'. (If he had said 'Last Net' it would have been an invitation for his nets to be lost).

The Vicar of Brighton was once entitled to a share as his tithe, in the profits from the fishing boats, so he had a good reason to bestow his blessing upon the enterprise at the start of the season.

The fine Sussex observer of folklore, Lillian Candlin, talked to one of the last fishermen to remember the custom being carried out. He told her that in the late nineteenth century the cost of the loaves would have been a penny-halfpenny each, bread and cheese sixpence-halfpenny, beer tuppence a pint, and the children's pop a penny-halfpenny a pint. Candling noted that the last time the custom was carried out was in Brighton in 1896.

BIRDS

AS with most natural creatures, birds figure largely in country folklore. The robin has always been a favourite in Sussex, and several legends have been woven around this neat little bird. For instance there is the charming story that while Christ was on the cross, a robin came and plucked a thorn from his crown, and was splashed on its breast with blood. Magpies, which are less popular birds, were said to carry a drop of Satan's blood on their tongues, as they also attended the crucifixion, but did nothing to help Jesus.

Still on the subject of the robin's red breast, there is also the story that they were the first to bring fire to mankind, thereby burning their breasts; or alternatively that they fetched water from Hell to help suffering man, and were burnt in the process – although why they should go to Hell for the water in the first place is not made clear.

Magpies have always been considered birds of ill omen, although a magpie on a roof is considered lucky, as it means that the house is in no danger of collapse; also a tree with a magpie nest will not fall (but only because the bird is in league with the Devil). However a magpie on an animal is thought to be a bad sign.

Even today most people know the magpie rhyme:

> *One means anger, two brings mirth,*
> *Three for a wedding, four for a birth,*
> *Five is Heaven, six is Hell,*
> *But seven's the very Devil himself.*

There are also variations on this rhyme.

Several other birds bring bad luck. The owl has been called a messenger of evil, and a raven is supposed to anticipate death. For more pleasant portents we must look to the swallows or house martins, who are said to bring good luck when first sighted. However you must not destroy the latter's nests on houses, as this will definitely bring bad luck, and the birds will never build on that house again.

Another rhyme well known in Sussex is:

> *Robins and wrens are God Almighty's friends,*
> *Martins and swallows are God Almighty's scholars.*

Sometimes the first line is rendered as 'Robins and wrens are God's little cocks and hens'.

The countryman was often captivated by the sounds of bird song. The great tit's two notes were said to sound like the blacksmith's hammer, and a chaffinch was said to sing, 'Will you, will you, kiss me dear'. There are many more similar sayings based on the sound of bird song.

A strange belief was that when someone was about to die a sound like the chirping of a bird may be heard. Feathers of game birds when mixed with the other feathers in a bed, were believed to prolong the death struggles of a dying person, so these were sometimes removed. Peacocks feathers indoors meant a death, or at the very least were unlucky. Clara Chandler, then aged eighty-nine, told me of this in 1980, but suggested that the belief was encouraged by the gentry, who wished their ornamental birds to be left alone.

Rooks were for many years associated with the Bishopric in Horsham, in fact this was often referred to as The Rookery, and the women who dwelt there as Rooks. Certainly the rook's nests in a group of trees in this road persisted during the whole of my childhood.

Collecting bird's eggs was considered a sure way to court bad luck. This was particularly so regarding robin's eggs, and if you take these then your fingers will grow crooked. But perhaps these tales were used to discourage boys from carrying out one of their favourite pastimes

There are many more legends and superstitions surrounding our feathered friends, and many of these tend to ignore county boundaries. The cuckoo has so many items of folklore attached to it, that he will appear in a separate entry later in this book.

MICHAEL BLANN

MICHAEL Blann was born in 1843 at Upper Beeding, the fifth child of sawyer Edward Blann and his wife Mary, who came from Poynings. When he was nine he was sent to work as a shepherd lad on the Sussex Downs, being paid the princely wage of three shillings and sixpence a week; so he must have received only rudimentary schooling.

He was interested in music from his earliest days, and we are told that his uncles were all good singers. He soon acquired a reputation as a singer himself, learning songs at sheep fairs, such as Findon, which he attended as part of his job. After the serious business of the day was done, the

Michael Blann

shepherds and others would gather to swop songs and stories.

By 1867 he had begun to write down his repertoire of songs in a notebook, and fortunately this has survived, and is now preserved in Worthing Museum, with his tin whistle. He also played the tin whistle and the jews harp, and was in demand as a singer and musician at harvest suppers and similar events.

He married Mary, a girl in service (just as most were at that time), although she was seven years his senior.

In his late sixties he went to live at Patching, but was still working as a shepherd. Mary died in 1914 at seventy-seven, and within eighteen months he married again, a seventy-three-year-old widow. She died in 1920, and Michael, now eighty-one, was determined not to be on his own, so he married for the third time – this time to a woman thirty years his junior. He died in February 1934 in his cottage.

Sussex has been fortunate in its Downland shepherds, many of them contributing to the preservation of the old ways of the county.

BLESSING THE SEA

THE customary time for blessing the sea, and fishing boats (also crops) is Rogationtide. Probably the best known Rogationtide ceremonies in Sussex are those carried out annually at Hastings, long associated with the Fishermen's Church of St Nicholas. This little church on the fishing beach dates from 1854 and although it is now a museum, church services are still held there. In 1894 the Reverend HJ Sanders became the chaplain to the Fishermen's Church, and presumably because he had once been a seaman he instituted the modern Blessing the Sea ceremony, which includes a procession from one of the Old Town churches, with a band and hymns such as *Eternal Father Strong to Save.*

Other similar ceremonies of blessing the sea, and the fishing boats, are carried on at Shoreham Beach and Lancing – see also Bending-in, on page 24.

Blessing the fishing boats at Lancing, 1992

BONFIRE NIGHT

The Fifth of November – Guy Fawkes Night – is the one night of the year when Sussex folk really let themselves go. Otherwise law-abiding citizens throw discretion to the wind and do things with blazing tar barrels and noisy fire crackers. Respectable tradespeople dress up in outlandish costumes and parade the streets; even the present-day fashion for religious ecumenism is forgotten for twenty-four hours as effigies of the Pope and 'No Popery' banners are carried in procession – at least in Lewes.

Why Sussex people should care so much for its bonfires and fireworks is not altogether clear. Certainly it has been suggested that Lewes, the otherwise peaceful county town, has particular memories to keep its anti-Guy Fawkes fervour alive – seventeen Protestant martyrs gave their lives here. But Lewes is by no means the only Sussex town that celebrates the Fifth with such abandon. It does appear that East Sussex (which was always a little more rowdy in its pleasures) shows slightly more enthusiasm than West, although this may be argued. Towns with particular Bonfire Night traditions include Battle, Rye, Hastings, Littlehampton, Billingshurst and Rotherfield; but most towns and villages celebrated in some degree, at least in the past.

Bonfires at this time of the year go back very much earlier than the Gunpowder Plot of 1605, but it is on record that the year following the abortive attempt, Lewes folk celebrated the non-event with a bonfire on Cliffe Hill. The custom of dragging flaming tar barrels along the streets soon became very much part of the Lewes celebrations, as did the street processions.

In the early part of the nineteenth century, the scenes enacted on November 5 each year at Lewes could be described only as wild and uncontrolled. In 1838, there was trouble and several arrests, and three years later, more than twenty people received prison sentences following attacks on the police. But worse was to come. In 1846 a mob piled tar barrels in front of the house of Mr Blackman, a Lewes magistrate, setting them alight and alarming those inside to such an extent that Mr Blackman went outside and requested the Bonfire Boys to disperse. He was met by jeers, and when he attempted to take one of the ringleaders into custody, he was set upon, and carried into the house senseless.

During the ensuing year, debate raged in local newspapers concerning the advisability or otherwise of curtailing Bonfire Night celebrations in the future. The authorities were plainly alarmed at what might happen in 1847 and prepared accordingly, with large numbers of police, including some from London. There were also no less than 170 Specials drawn from the local tradespeople, although many were reluctant to become too closely involved.

The Bonfire Boys had no intention of giving up easily and on the big night in 1847, the riotous scenes culminated with Lord Chichester addressing the crowds from the steps of County Hall, and ordering them to go home before the police cleared the streets. But this was not the end of the story. For the rest of November, mobs gathered in the High Street after dark with fireworks and tar barrels. Once more Specials were sworn in, and eventually calm was restored to the town. In more modern times the celebrations became better organised and the separate Bonfire Societies emerged. Yet it would be foolish to suppose that Lewes on November 5 is a town for the faint-hearted. As George Townsend of Lewes told me, on Guy Fawkes Night you never wore anything but your oldest clothes, and you set out expecting the worst and if possible wearing a pair of goggles, which were very popular each year in Lewes. In 1904 the firework named after the town the 'Lewes Rouser', was officially banned, and in 1905 the custom of dragging fiery tar barrels through the streets, and hurling them into the river, was also banned – although blazing barrels remain a feature of the Lewes celebration. Some shops still board up their windows, and a certain amount of damage and rowdyism inevitably takes place.

Many Sussex people took rather a pride in the activities that went on each year in the otherwise sleepy town. One spoke of 'a party of young men, dressed in farmers' smocks, singing *Sussex by the Sea* with great abandon. Another told me of how her grandfather dressed as a devil, and secreted pins in his tail 'so that when people tried to pull it, they pricked themselves'.

But in this brief account, I must move on from Lewes, to other parts of the county, where Sussex folk also looked upon November 5 as a night when 'anything goes', although in East Sussex, there are virtually no other celebrations *on* the Fifth as town and village bonfire society members (including many from West Sussex) are in Lewes. So the others' celebrations are on different dates, starting with East Hoathly and Halland on August Bank Holiday and ending towards the end of November

The *West Sussex Gazette* of November 12, 1863, carried an impassioned letter from a reader concerning the boys living in the vicinity of a country house close to the South Downs. On the Fifth, the occupants of the house were aroused at 8am by seven small boys with paper caps on their heads, brandishing cow horns. After reciting their Bonfire Hymn they blew a flourish on their horns, and then had to be driven away by force. An hour later, three big boys arrived dressed in the same manner and with blackened faces, and repeated the performance. They also had a 'guy' with them, which they planted before the front door, invoking curses upon it. This sort of thing continued throughout the morning, and was taken up again in the evening. The writer ended with the pious hope that the 'plough boys and yokels' may soon learn that nearly all England has given up such mummery. Apparently Sussex was maintaining its old traditions longer than elsewhere, just as it has often done.

All this smacks of an even earlier origin than the Gunpowder Plot, akin to mummers, plough boys and wassailers. Many of the Bonfire Night celebrations are of a very basic kind – a desire to break loose from the bonds of convention, on at least one night of the year.

The search for burnable material can also cause a good deal of trouble. Helena Hall of Lindfield recalled the story of an elderly man who urged the boys to 'pile em on' as heavy bundles of faggots were thrown to the flames. Not until the following day did he discover that the faggots were his own property, brought from the back of his house, whilst he cheered them on at the front.

When the Lindfield tollgates were removed in 1884, both gates were burnt on a big bonfire on November 5, and on another occasion Miss Hall's own gate was ripped from its hinges and her fence torn up to help swell one of the fires in the High Street.

At Rye, Bonfire Night was considered a very appropriate time for practical jokes. Once they put a man up to his neck in a tar barrel, and barrels filled with burning tar were rolled down Conduit Hill, and shopkeepers boarded up their shop-fronts as the town prepared for a state of voluntary siege.

Mr R Goatcher, the market gardener of Washington, told me of a Bonfire Night he remembered from his boyhood in East Preston. The one local policeman had been called to Littlehampton, leaving

Crawley High Street in November 1914, and the last November 5 bonfire to be built in the roadway.

East Preston unguarded by the law. Enboldened by this state of affairs the local lads decided to roll tar barrels up the road to start a bonfire in front of Preston Cottage. At the crossroads they gathered all the burnable material they could find (the policeman's included). One woman brought out a cradle, saying she would have no further use for it. The result was a tremendous fire which was still burning the next morning, to such an extent that the carters had a problem in getting their horses round the corner.

At Hastings Museum they have the banner of the Hastings Borough Bonfire Society, dating from the time when the Hastings celebrations vied in size and scale with those at Lewes and Battle. The banner is of painted canvas 8ftx12ft. They also have a guy's head of the Bohemia Bonfire Society – apparently the heads of the guys were too valuable to be burnt and were taken off the effigies at the last moment and retained for future use.

Henry Burstow of Horsham tells us that in the early 1870s the Horsham Bonfire Night celebrations were some of the best in the country. He said that the size and content varied through the years; the periods of decline and revival being in accordance with the enthusiasm of the inhabitants, and the opposition or indifference of the magistrates. Sometimes there were as many as three separate fires (the largest always in the Carfax), with others in the Bishopric and Collyer's School. Several parties toured the town during the day, each with its own guy. In 1870, Horsham Bonfire Boys Society was formed, and affairs became better organised, with huge guys ten or twelve feet high paraded round the town.

At Crawley, the bonfire was also held in the main street, until it had to be moved because the road surface was suffering greatly.

At Rye in the 1860s/70s, November 5 was a day of riots and merrymaking. One street bonfire was nearly responsible for the destruction of the old Cinque Ports Hotel. Boats were burnt, irrespective of ownership, and unpopular people were burnt in effigy, with disguises concealing the identities of the ringleaders. It was an unlucky day for anyone unwise enough to upset the Bonfire Boys.

At little Billingshurst, a man dressed as a devil ran up the side of the bonfire, and was obliged to run down as soon as the fire was lit. One year he was badly burnt and the tradition ended.

At Slaugham things were said to be 'pretty wild'. WH Kensett wrote in 1929 that the day started off with men shouting 'Holla boys, holla boys, and God save the King. Holla boys, holla boys, and let the bells ring'. The church bells were then rung merrily, and apparently no faggot, stack, box or barrel was safe from the fire. A tall pole in the centre of the fire was known as 'the scrag', and when the fire had burnt down, this was carted around on the men's shoulders to the pubs. Where it ended up was said to be 'wropped in mystery'.

In 1888 in Bognor on November 15 (the Prince of Wales' birthday) up to 3,000 people watched the monster bonfire on the sands, with contingents from Arundel, Chichester and Littlehampton joining in.

This list could go on and on, but one more example must suffice. At Westfield on November 5 in 1908, the windmill was burnt down. And who do you think they blamed? Why, the Bonfire Boys of course.

BOSHAM

BOSHAM (pronounced Bos-ham) is a magical place, even today – at least it always seems so to me, and I believe I am not alone. Legends abound, such as that it was a monk by the name of Dicul who actually brought Christianity to Sussex with a small monastery at Bosham, pre-dating St Wilfrid.

Possibly the best known Bosham story is of King Canute who was supposed to have ordered the waves on this shore to retreat, in order to teach his courtiers a lesson (although it has to be admitted that several other places also claim this honour).

Canute was said to have lived here, and that his daughter was buried in the lovely little church. It was fervently believed by many old Bosham folk that the eight-year-old princess was interred inside the church. During its restoration in the nineteenth century, the Reverend Henry Mitchell investigated the site said to be her tomb. The floor was taken up on August 4, 1865, and the doubters were

The village of Bosham, part of Chichester Harbour, with the church of Holy Trinity (which appears on the Bayeaux Tapestry) dominating the waterfront buildings

silenced when a small coffin was unearthed. The lid, when removed, disclosed the remains of a child of about the right age. The coffin was also said to correspond with Canute's period. After being on show for a time it was then closed and reburied. In 1954 the coffin was again investigated, although no bones were disclosed, implying that the earlier opening had caused them to disintegrate. A small bottle containing some brown liquid was found at that time, and this became something of a mystery, as it had not been mentioned at the time of the earlier dig. During the 1954 events, a another larger coffin made of Horsham stone was found three feet away from the smaller one. In it were the bones of a well-built man of around sixty. This tied in with another local tradition that Earl Godwin, King Harold's father, was buried here.

Many people will know of Bosham because it was from here that Harold sailed on his ill-fated voyage to Normandy in 1064, and because the church appears on the famous Bayeux tapestry.

One of the most fascinating Bosham legends concerns the church bells. In the days when the Norse pirates made raids on this part of the country, a band pillaged the church, seizing one of the bells, and ignoring the pleas of the villagers. The bells that remained were rung as a curse on the vandals, and at once the stolen bell broke loose and crashed through the deck of the ship. It sank in the water at a spot now known as 'Bell Hole', and there it remained. However,the story does not end there, as the old folk will tell you that when the remaining bells are rung, the missing one will ring in unison with them. As is usual with these sunken bell legends, the story goes on to relate that a witch once told the villagers that their bell could be recovered if attempts were made to pull it up by means of a team of completely white oxen. But one beast had a tuft of black hair not spotted by the witch, and consequently the ropes snapped and the bell sank back beneath the waves.

The Bosham authority, the Reverend KH MacDermott, writing in 1926, said that there was still within living memory the 'sluggard-wakers wand' preserved in the church.This was used by the parish clerk to rap anyone on the head who was unwise enough to nod off during one of the interminably long sermons. Also in the church was once preserved what was said to be the staff of Bevis, the legendary Sussex giant, who could stride across Bosham Harbour in one bound.

*Bosham stone coffins.One may have contained
the bones of Canute's daughter*

One more of Bosham's many legends tells that Cavalier jewels and cash from Civil War days are buried in the Manor House. This building also houses several ghosts, including one of an old man who died sitting at a window awaiting the return of his son after they had quarrelled. The Manor House also has the almost obligatory story of a secret tunnel linking it with the church.

Yet another tradition has it that when a bride of good reputation was married in Bosham church, a salute was fired from a gun on Quay Meadow, although this custom ceased in the 1880s.

Bosham had its own gang of Christmas mummers, or tipteers, as they were known in Sussex. They came out on Boxing Day, wearing Sussex smocks and 'chummies' (round black felt hats). They performed at various stops on the way to Chichester, ending there in the evening, probably a little bit the worse for wear, but very happy.

BRANDY BALL MAN

Brandy Balls as big as St Pauls,
Who will buy my Brandy Balls.

THIS was said to be the distinctive call of sellers of this once popular confection in the streets of Brighton in the late nineteenth century. My particular knowledge of the Brandy Ball Man comes from my mother, who recited the above rhyme to me when I was a youngster. She claimed to remember him (or them – assuming there was more than one). However this seems uncertain, as she was born in 1889, and according to correspondents in the *Sussex County Magazine* in the 1940s, the Brandy Ball sellers were active in Brighton in the 1860/70s, so perhaps my mother's recollections stemmed from memories passed on to her by her parents or grandparents. One account said that the Brandy Ball Man was an Italian aristocrat, tall and very clean, in a white apron and bearing a glass covered tray hanging from his neck. He is said to have attracted customers by whistling like a bird, and he was not known to have used any spoken call. More than likely there were a number of Brandy Ball merchants around the same period, as another recollection is of a German, who was fat and not particularly tall. This man's call was said to be 'Brandy Balls, oh so nice'. Another writer said that in the 1880s the seller was known as Old Dizzy, on account of his resemblance to Disraeli. His cry was 'Oh, they are beautiful today, ladies; they are so fine'. Someone also recalled a painting of a Brandy Ball Man in a white apron and a red cap, bearing a tray of sweets, and with Brighton's Chain Pier in the background. The most likely scenario would appear to be that in the period when this sweet was popular, there were several sellers active in Brighton, with slightly different calls.

BREDE OGRE

BREDE has a very nasty legend of a flesh-eating giant known as The Ogre, who reputably preyed on children – in fact he was particularly fond of one for his nightly feast. He was usually referred to as 'Old Oxenbridge', although there is some doubt as to which member of the Oxenbridge family was meant. The favourite candidate is Sir Goddard Oxenbridge, who lived in the sixteenth century, although history, as opposed to folklore, tells us that he was a good Christian, who now lies in effigy in Brede church.

The legendary giant was finally thwarted by the children themselves who doped him with drink, and once he was senseless, proceeded to saw him in half with a wooden saw. This is supposed to have happened at Stubb's Lane, between Brede Place and the church, at a place known as Groaning Bridge. The spot is said to be haunted by a ghost of the legendary giant.

Some doubt has been expressed as to whether Sir Goddard was in fact larger than average, as his statue in the church is quite small. Edmund Austen in his book *Brede, The Story of a Sussex Parish* (1946), mentions that a local man remembered excavations being carried out in the Oxenbridge chancel, when a skull of enormous size was unearthed.

Mothers of naughty children were said to have used the story to encourage better behaviour, and smugglers were said to have used it to scare villagers away from their activities.

Brede Place has an alternative name of The Giant's House, which adds a little credence to the tale. There are several ghost stories attached to the house, including one of a priest, who is supposed to have used the chapel.

BULL BAITING

FROM 1700 to 1834 it was customary for bulls to be baited by dogs before being slaughtered, as it was believed to make the meat more tender. The practice was abolished by the efforts of the Earl of Egremont in 1835.

In the 1890s Mr Cramp of Horsham played cricket as a boy in traffic-free West Street. Then for a change the boys would stop and say 'let's find the old bull ring on the Carfax'. They would then scratch in the grass until they discovered it, half buried.

Although it was not made illegal until 1835, bull baiting actually ceased in Horsham following 1813. Between the two world wars the ring was preserved as a curiosity, still on the Carfax but surrounded by low railings, close to the old stocks and whipping post. Later it was removed to the museum.

Horsham stories tell of bulls that were so fond of being baited that they were known to find their own way from Chesworth Farm to the Carfax. On the other hand there are other tales, rather more believable, of the bulls who escaped, causing the spectators to climb trees. Bulldogs or bull-terriers (or any other vicious breeds) were used, and if after half an hour or so the bull had not been killed, it was despatched and the meat cut up and sold in Butchers Row (later known as Middle Street), or even given to the poor.

At the last baiting in 1813, the ring was obscured by dirt and grease, so the custom was evidently virtually extinct by that time. When some humane individuals endeavoured to bring it to a permanent end, they had to endure some anger from rougher members of the community.

Bulls were baited at many places in Sussex, the favourite day for the 'sport' being St Thomas' Day (December 21). In 1810 a Sussex newspaper thought it newsworthy enough to report that a bull had been tied to a stake and baited at Hove on Easter Tuesday. On this occasion the animal broke loose and charged the spectators, and the baiting was then called off. Previously the Annual Bull Bait had been on Hove Fair Day.

At Alfriston in 1784 the baiting was accompanied by an added attraction of a 'grand balloon ascent' at four in the afternoon. We are told that the best dog in the baiting was presented with a handsome collar valued at fifteen shillings.

Brighton carried on with its baiting up to the middle of the nineteenth century, and at Chichester many bulldogs were kept in the town just for the baitings. At Hassocks in 1788, John Burgess, a strict Baptist tradesman from Ditchling, noted in his diary: 'Went to Friars Oak for a bull bait to sell my dog. I selled him for one guinea on condition he was hurt; but as he received no hurt, I took him home again. I had all my expences paid as I had a dog there.'

Many other places in Sussex have records of bull baiting, including Lewes, Rottingdean (in front of the White Horse Inn), Battle, Henfield and Petworth. After the

Bull ring at Horsham Carfax, 1930s

practice ceased the rings appear to have been overlooked, until somewhat later they were discovered and treated as curiosities. At Henfield the post was dug up by a road mender in Golden Square, and at Rye Hill close to the Kings Head Hotel, the ring could be seen long after the baitings had ceased. At Rye the remains of the bull ring used at Beggars Bush fair on the feast of St Bartholomew could be seen in a field close to the Kings Head Hotel.

A more pleasant reminder of a very unpleasant custom is a pottery group at Wilmington Priory, which depicts a bull baiting scene.

BURIAL AT A CROSSROADS

THIS barbaric custom was intended as a deterrent to the idea of ultimate resurrection, in the case of a poor wretch who had taken his or her own life. Thomas Hood in his *Faithless Nelly Gray* wrote: 'And they buried him in four cross roads, with a stake in his inside'.

A typical example of the custom occurred in 1679 at Lewes when Robert Brinkhurst poisoned his friend William Moor. When the accused was being questioned, he swallowed a quantity of yellow arsenic and died after great pains lasting from Tuesday to Saturday. He was refused Christian burial and was taken in a dung cart, without a coffin, to the crossroads near Spital Barn, and there flung into a hole dug north and south; a stake having first been driven through the uncovered corpse.

Mark Antony Lower, writing in 1854, told the following story. At Chalvington, a miller described as 'the only honest miller ever known', failed in his business and in a fit of despair hanged himself in his own mill He was buried as custom instructed, in a neighbouring crossway, an oak stake having been driven through his body. This was then said to grow into a tree, which threw out a single shrivelled branch across the road – the only one it ever produced. The spot was, of course, haunted, although the stories were considered mere folklore until, some time later, a labourer digging sand near the roots of the tree, found a human skeleton.

A *Sussex County Magazine* contributor in 1930 told how there had been a gibbet at the crossroads leading to the Downs, opposite the modern Goring Road. The bodies of felons executed there were denied the rites of the church and burial in consecrated ground. Such spots became known as 'Dead Man's Acre' or 'Heathen Burial Ground'.

Also in the *Sussex County Magazine,* in 1953, a story was told of how a man named Steere robbed the mail at Durrington and was hanged at the crossroads, where he was also buried. Then it became known as 'Steere's Bank', and many years later a water main being laid through the village disclosed human bones at the cross roads, assumed to be those of the unfortunate Steere.

Still from the *Sussex County Magazine* there is the legend that surrounds a mound at Warnham. About 140 years ago a young soldier, who had been crossed in love, hanged himself close by; and

Goring cross roads in the early 1900s

in accordance with the custom of the times was buried near the crossroads. The story then becomes even more interesting, as it was believed that the grave was kept in constant order with fresh flowers planted from year to year, although no one was ever able to discover who was responsible. The soldier being a stranger to the village would not have had any relatives there, and it was suggested that gypsies passing through may have been the donors of the flowers. Another version of the tale states that it was actually a cattle stealer's grave. He was hanged on a tree near the crossroads, and after a grave was dug underneath him, he was cut down and dropped straight in. Apparently children put flowers on the grave, and the roadman Sugar Woodman trimmed it once a year.

HENRY BURSTOW

HENRY Burstow (1826-1916) appears several times in these pages, as I quote from his wonderful little book *Reminiscences of Horsham,* originally published in 1911. Although his name does not appear anywhere in the book, it was the Horsham historian William Albery (1865-1950) who made the book possible, as he noted down Burstow's vast store of memories from his long life in Horsham, including a great many of the towns's oral traditions which otherwise would not have been preserved.

It was also Albery, together with a group of his friends, who

Henry Burstow

instigated the publication and sale of the book.

Burstow was a cobbler, bell ringer, songster and local celebrity, although it has to be said that many of his contemporaries did not always approve of him. He lived in the town all his life, never sleeping away from home. He never earned more than twelve shillings and sixpence a week, and late in life faced the spectre of the workhouse. It was the publication of his *Reminiscences* and some other activities by William Albery and those of similar outlook, that made it possible for Henry and his wife to remain in their cottage until the grand old man died in his 90th year.

Henry Burstow was particularly noted as a great singer of old songs, his repertoire running to 500 (and probably many more). The folk song collectors Ralph Vaughan Williams, and Lucy Broadwood, gathered many gems from his vast store, although his repertoire also included many items of doubtful value, but as with most traditional singers, all was grist to his mill. In 1906, when he was 80, he sang 110 songs on forty-one consecutive evenings to his patient wife. At 82 he was honoured by the town, being invited to sing with the Horsham Recreation Band at the Kings Head Assembly Rooms (March 12, 1908). Included were two of his best songs *The Gallant Poacher* and *In Bristol Town*.

As Mr and Mrs Garner told me, he was always 'an old fashioned sort of man' and his reputation was of someone slightly unusual. He had a number of eccentricities. For instance he had a taste for odd scraps of knowledge, which he would store away in his mind, bringing them out when the occasion seemed appropriate, such as when he wanted to entertain children.

In the late 1950s I became interested in tracking down information concerning Burstow, and found that at that time there were still Horsham folk alive who remembered him, I was told how he delighted in being asked to sing, and how he never missed an opportunity to learn fresh songs. Charlie Potter told me of Burstow visiting his father in order to swap songs, while the youngster sat under the kitchen table taking it all in.

Mr Pratt lent me Burstow's own notebook, which included notable events in Horsham's history, quite different from the entries in a standard type of book. For instance how in 1826 William Verrall (known as Lad) walked fifty miles a day for twenty days; and when it was so cold in January 1833 that the tea cups froze to the saucer at breakfast. Burstow's idea of entertainment was in walking to Newdigate in Surrey on Saturday nights, arriving there at about 4pm and change ringing the church bells until 10pm. Then on to the the pub to sing until midnight, then walking back to Horsham, arriving there at about 2am.

His delightful book became a much sought-after collectors item, and in 1975 I was able to arrange for a reprint to be published in America, as no British publisher was interested. This reprint, with a lengthy new introduction, was quickly snapped up, and now the reprint has become almost as rare as the original. Perhaps reading this, someone will feel impelled to undertake a new reprint of the work, so that the memories of this incredible man may once again come to life.

CAROLS

SUSSEX is fortunate in being able to claim one of the most popular Christmas carols as its own. *The Sussex Carol,* also known by its first line *On Christmas Night all Christians Sing,* was collected by Ralph Vaughan Williams from Mrs Verrall of Monks Gate on May 24, 1904, when she was about 50. The young composer noted several songs from Mrs Verrall and her husband around this time. She died in 1918, and her husband a few years later, after they had moved from Monks Gate to Horsham. They had three children, and I was able to talk to one son several years ago, and heard from him his memories of Vaughan Williams and a group of other 'gentlemen' who visited his parents with a phonograph, to record their songs.

Another folk song collector was Lucy Broadwood of Rusper, and she noted the *Sussex Mummers Carol* (O Mortal Man Remember Well) around 1876-81. The band of Christmas mummers (or tipteerers) from the neighbourhood of Horsham visited the Broadwood home at Lyne, Rusper, and Lucy Broadwood recalled how 'they clustered together, wooden swords in hand, at the close of their play St George and the Turk', and sang, wholly unconscious of the contrast between the solemnity of the carol and the grotesqueness of their appearance, for they wore dresses of coloured calico, and old 'chimney pot hats, heavily trimmed with shreds of ribbon, gaudy paper fringes and odd ornaments'.

Sussex mummers often incorporated their favourite carols into the close of their plays, a popular one being *The Moon Shines Bright.* The Compton Mummers used *I Saw Three Ships,* which included some very secular lines such as 'He did whistle and she did sing' and 'Jack be nimble and Jack be quick'.

Several Sussex villages had their own carols, written by local amateur musicians usually associated with the church choir. The Ditchling carol *Be Merry All* was composed by Peter Parsons (1825-1901), who was the parish clerk, and who used an old wooden pitchpipe to start the choir. Peter was a local character, and the village 'snob' (shoemaker), who lived in a wooden bungalow.

The Burwash carol *Hail Happy Morn* was sung on Christmas morning between 3 and 4am, in the late nineteenth century. It was probably written by James Fleming of Burwash (1805-1872) or perhaps his father. He was described as an organist, hairdresser, barber, book-binder, harmonium maker, tuner and violinist – so the composition of a carol must have been an easy task for one so multi-talented.

The Stanmer carol *Come Hail the Glorious Morn* was popular in the village in the mid nineteenth century, the tune having been composed by S Wakeley. Falmer also had its own local carol, *See Seraphic Throngs*, although the composer is not known.

We can also claim the man known as 'the Carol King' as a Sussex celebrity. This was John Mason Neale, one time Vicar of Crawley, and later Warden of Sackville College, East Grinstead.

The Falmer Carol, See Seraphic Throngs, harmonised by the Rev KH MacDermott, Rector of Buxted, and decorated by Frederick Jones

He was responsible for publishing *Good King Wenceslas, O Come, O Come Emmanuel, Good Christian Men Rejoice* and *A Great and Mighty Wonder.* In 1853 the publication of his collection, *Carols for Christmas,* led to a revival in carol singing. Seventy-two of his hymns appear in *The English Hymnal.*

Christina Rosetti often stayed at Aldwick Lodge, near Bognor, and it was one Christmas visit there that inspired her to write the words of the lovely carol *In the Bleak Midwinter.*

CATS

UNDOUBTEDLY there were once wild cats roaming the Sussex woods, just as there were wolves, wild boars and perhaps even dragons, if legends are to be believed. The last definite record of a Sussex wild cat concerned one said to have been sighted in Rogate Forest in 1782 – although many other claims were made long after that. Even within living memory of the 1960s, there was said to have been a wild cat responsible for sheep killings, living in a hide-out not far from Rottingdean High Street.

In more recent times there have been persistent reports of 'big cats' being seen throughout Sussex. Many of these may relate to feral cats – farm or domestic cats which have become wild, or even an animal such as a raccoon which had escaped from a private zoo.

Some of the reports are more difficult to explain, and this also applies to similar sightings in other counties. The press love these stories of what are often referred to as pumas, or just 'big cats'. Here are just a few of the sightings, and readers must decide whether they are zoological, supernatural or just fanciful.

In the 1960s many sightings of cats, said to be twice the size of domestic animals, were made in the Plaistow, Rogate and Chiddingfold areas. In 1975 a puma-like animal crossed the path of two girls riding near Horsham. Two days later at Peas Pottage a woman reported seeing a puma sitting near the M23 motorway. In the 1980s it was the turn of a publican at Binstead, near Arundel to see a 'big cat', and it was during this same period that the press carried stories concerning 'the Beast of Yapton'.

Coming up to the early 1990s a 'big cat' was reported from East Grinstead, and in 1992 at least two residents of Shoreham spotted a 'Sussex Puma' near the beach. The newspaper story also mentioned other Sussex sightings from Hove, Storrington, Bognor, Hassocks and Henfield. The most recent story I have seen concerns a puma on the prowl in Adversane in 1998, when a motorist reported it to the police – although the RSPCA said they had received no information about it.

Like UFOs and crop circles, we must file these stories under 'Unexplained' and await the verdict of time as to how important within the realm of Sussex folklore they really are.

But to end the section on cats, I really must give a mention to the

Henfield's Cat House in the 1930s

locally famous Cat House of Henfield. The story goes back to the nineteenth century when Canon Nathaniel Woodard (founder of the famous Woodard Schools) lived in Henfield. Close by lived a true Sussex eccentric, Robert 'Bob' Ward in a house known as The Leeches. The two men just couldn't agree, and their mutual dislike came to a head when a cat owned by the Canon killed Bob's canary. Because of this outrage, the canary's owner made black cut-out effigies of the cat with a canary in its paws, and hung these around the house, causing them to rattle whenever the Canon passed by. He also arranged a collection of scallop shells, which he jangled at the same time, and even fired off a wooden canon. Much of this commotion annoyed other neighbours as much as the Canon, and eventually Bob Ward was persuaded to modify his feud.

No doubt about it Ward was a genuine eccentric, as he used altar boards stolen from the local church as the head and foot boards of his bed. After his death they were rescued and returned to the church. The story of the cats may have been a newspaper exaggeration, but it has certainly passed into local folklore, and modern replicas may be still be seen on the cottage for those who care to look.

CATTERING AND CLEMMENING

THE feast day of St Catherine, virgin and martyr, is kept on November 25, and that of St Clement, Pope and martyr, two days earlier on November 23. The two have often been linked in a folk custom known as Clemmening (or Clemming) and Cattering (there are alternative spellings). Sussex children used these feast days as an excuse to beg for fruit or pennies, the connection with the saints giving the whole thing a semblance of respectability. They sang:

> *Cathern and Clemmen be here, here, here.*
> *Give us your apples and give us your beer.*
> *One for Peter, one for Paul,*
> *Three for him who made us all.*
>
> *Clemmen was a good man,*
> *Cathern was his Mother.*
> *Give me your best and not your worst,*
> *And God will give your soul good rest.*

The adult's view of these antics seems to have varied. At one time, children were given a half-holiday to celebrate the feasts, although in 1540 a proclamation was issued to the effect that 'Neither children should be decked nor go about upon St Nicholas, St Catherine, St Clement, the Holy Innocents, or such-like days'.

St Clement's Day was also an important day for blacksmiths in Sussex, as they claimed him as their patron saint (fishermen make a similar claim - and tradition says that he was martyrd by being thrown into the sea tied to an anchor).

The blacksmiths celebrated by a feast, presided over by an effigy of 'Old Clem', in fact the custom itself was often referred to as 'Old Clem's Night'. The most important part of the feast was provided by a way-goose (a leg of pork stuffed with onions). Mr Laker of Brighton told me in the 1950s: 'In Storrington, when I was at school, the village blacksmith used to fire a gun in his anvil (*sic*) and then have a supper in the evening at The Anchor. They called it Old Clem Night, and my father and uncle used to go each year after the corn sowing season was over. The carters had bread and cheese given them by the village blacksmith.' Note the mention of firing the anvil which traditionally was always carried out on this particular day of the year.

At Burwash 'Old Clem' (an effigy with wig, beard and pipe) was set up over the door of the inn for the smith's feast. Similar customs were observed at Bramber, and many other places. During the evening toasts were drunk, one to Vulcan:

A rural smithy of Edwardian days, this one at Hadlow Down

> *Here's to Vulcan, as bold as a lion,*
> *A large shop and no iron,*
> *A big hearth, and no coal,*
> *And a large pair of bellows full of holes.*

Another popular toast was 'True hearts and sound bottoms, chequered shirts and leather aprons'. During the meal there would be songs, the most popular being the blacksmith's particular favourite, 'Twankydillo':

> *Here's a health to the jolly blacksmith, the best of all fellows,*
> *Who works at his anvil while the boy blows the bellows,*
> *For it makes his bright hammer to rise and to fall,*
> *Here's to Old Cole, and to Young Cole, and to Old Cole of all.*
> *Twankydillo, twankydillo, twankydillo, dillo, dillo, dillo.*
> *With a roaring paid of blowpipes made from the green willow.*

CAVES

LIKE tunnels and hidey-holes, caves attract folklore whenever and wherever they exist. Possibly the best known caves in Sussex are the extensive underground chambers at Hastings. Tradition connects these to the Romans or Danes, and, in more modern times to smugglers. The earliest published picture of the caves was in *The Gentleman's Magazine* in 1786, although their modern history is said to have begun when in 1825 a man working in his garden, drove his spade through the rock, and Hastings' greatest tourist attractions were re-discovered. During the following century poor families are supposed to have lived in the caves, and in the early part of the l900s soldiers used them for gambling.

Figures carved within the caves included St Clement, Wellington, Napoleon and a Hastings smuggler. Attractions mentioned in local guide books include a Roman bath, the chapel, the hole in the wall and the ballroom. During the Second World War the caves were used as air-raid shelters and drawings of Montgomery and Churchill survive from this era. As well as smugglers, local inn-keepers were said to have used the caves for storing goods which had eluded the attention of the authorities.

From Seaford there is the story of two large caves called Puck's Parlours. These were reached from the cliff top by a narrow, dangerous path. The last man to enter them was said to be Tom Cheale, who went down with a rope to obtain three young peregrine falcons in 1881.

Isfield gives us the story of a cave in the rocks at Buckham Hill. This was the home of old Moggy Mothballs, a local celebrity who trundled her belongings around in an old pram. She wore several coats, donated to her by well-wishers, one on top of the other. When she died a small fortune in notes was said to have been found sewn into the linings of the coats.

Rottingdean, with its many stories of smuggling, has one concerning some caves in the chalk cliffs facing the beach, one of which was secured by an iron door. The tradition was of an underground passage reached through this door, leading to the old vicarage in the village.

One of the best Sussex cave stories concerns Parson Darby's Hole, at the base of Belle-Tout, near Birling Gap. A local legend says that the hole existed long before Parson Darby's time (around 1715), and that this had always been used by smugglers. However the best known story tells of how Jonathan Darby, Vicar of Eastdean, excavated a cave and staircase, as a refuge for shipwrecked sailors. He visited the hole on stormy nights, hanging out a lantern to attract those who might need help. Tradition says that he once rescued twelve Dutch sailors in this way, and on another occasion, the entire crew of a brig with twenty-three hands. One wonders how the parson's flock viewed his efforts, when many of them must have gained a living off the spoils of shipwrecks.

A twist to the story is provided by another local account that says that Darby excavated the cave in order to escape from the temper of his wife. However when she died in December 1723 he was said to have described his home as desolate, and on their joint grave he speaks of 'my Beloved Anne', so the stories of her temper may have been a fabrication.

A correspondent in the *Sussex County Magazine* in 1944 recalled that his brother as a boy climbed down into the cave. He found a rope hanging down, and when he pulled it, it held fast. As a boy the author Arthur Beckett climbed into the hole by means of a rope (the same one?), but by 1909 the cave was said to be almost non-existent. The story of Parson Darby and his locally famous hole was very popular in Victorian times, and even sparked off poems. Someone of a less romantic frame of mind pointed out that the brethren of Trinity House had a number of caves excavated in the vicinity for rescue purposes, although there appear to be no record of these.

An early picture of Parson Darby's Hole with two young adventurers

CELEBRATION ARCHES

THEY really knew how to celebrate in Victorian times. No juggernauts or double decker buses to worry about, in fact not a lot of traffic at all. Hence the wonderful idea of decorated arches across the roads – often at the main entrances to the towns or villages where an important event or visit was planned.

Chichester seems to have made a habit of erecting these arches, which were perhaps inspired by the four original city gates. These were pulled down in 1773, apart from the east gate which remained until 1783. (On Hock Monday the gatekeepers kept their gates closed, charging a penny to open them – which they kept.)

In l902 arches on the sites of the old city gates were erected to mark the coronation of Edward V11. Again in 1910 similar arches appeared for the coronation of George V. These were full size structures of wood and canvas, two of them being lit by hanging lanterns. In 1911 the most grand arch was at the site of the south gate, as this was the road to the railway station.

Ceremonial arches were also popular in Bognor. In 1897 for the Diamond Jubilee of Queen Victoria, a triumphal arch was built in London Road. Again in July 1900 an arch appeared to mark the

A celebration arch at Chichester, 1910

Another Chichester arch, this one from 1887,
celebrating Victoria's Golden Jubilee

opening by the Duchess of York of the Princess Mary Homes. In 1906 it was the turn of the High street to have its arch to celebrate a royal visit to the town. And again in 1910 the coronation of George V was marked in the same way.

In Arundel arches likened to the castle were built in wood and canvas; in 1902 to mark the return of Henry, Duke of Norfolk from the South African War, and again in 1904 when the same duke brought his bride Gwendolen home to the castle.

Villages also celebrated with arches. At Walberton a coronation arch was built as late as 1937 on the green, paid for by public subscription. This was of oak, although eventually the timbers became unsafe, and the structure was rebuilt in 1980, with an inscription reading, 'Erected in 1937. Restored 1980'.

CHANCTONBURY RING

CALLED The Monarch of the Sussex Hills, and also the most mysterious place in Sussex, Chanctonbury Ring is 700 feet above sea level, and has a view stretching more than 300 miles on a clear day. This is probably the Sussex spot with more traditions and folklore than any other. Ancient history speaks of an ancient fort, Celtic earthworks and a Roman temple, so it is not surprising that a great many old beliefs are attached to the ring.

Local people will tell you that it is impossible to count the trees on Chanctonbury, although it has also been said that there are actually 365 of them. That was before the great storm of 1987, which changed the top of the ring, just as it did so many other places in southern England.

A persistent belief is that birds will not sing there, but this is said about many well-wooded places in Sussex. The crown of beech trees was the work in 1760 of Charles Goring of Wiston House. When he was eighty-five he told in a poem how he planted the trees, toiling up the hill daily, and carrying water to nurture the young plants.

The Devil, too, has to have a hand in the origins of the ring, just as he has in so many Sussex things. When he was digging the Dyke (*ibid*) he threw up clods of earth, which became the ring. He also had enough left over to become the Isle of Wight in the Solent.

Chanctonbury Ring before the Great Storm of 1987

Chanctonbury Ring has a long association with witchcraft, ghosts, unseen forces and even UFO sightings. Fairies also frequent the ring, dancing there on certain nights of the year, and in particular on Midsummer's Eve.

The most enduring legend says that if you walk twelve times (some versions have it as seven), at midnight on either May Day Eve, Midsummer's Eve, Midsummer's Night, or any moonlit night, then the Devil will appear and offer you a bowl of soup (sometimes this is porridge, or even milk). There is one condition – you must move round the ring backwards, or anti-clockwise (widdershins is the Sussex expression for this). If you accept the Devil's meal, then he will take possession of your soul. (This moving in a circle has often been likened to ancient dances which may once have been performed on this most magical site.) Unlike many Sussex legends which now surface only in written accounts, the story of the Devil and his bowl of soup (like the Devil's Dyke legend) is still heard from the mouths of Sussex folk themselves.

Ghosts seen here include those of a druid, and a royal astrologer. There have also been sightings of men on galloping horses, perhaps Julius Caesar and his armies. Sometimes there is nothing to be seen, just the sound of horses galloping, and drums being beaten. Until 1866, when a ploughman turned up an Anglo-Saxon silver hoard close by, there was also a persistent ghost of a bearded ancient walking around searching for treasure. In modern times UFOs are said to have been sighted here, and black magic rituals have been carried out.

Undoubtedly it is a place where many people find difficulty in remaining after nightfall. Some students in 1967 were said to have fled before dawn, although they had intended to stay the night to take photographs and make tapes. Dr Philip Gosse, the author, who lived at Wiston in the 1930s, believed that the ring was haunted, and he had no wish to repeat a night time visit. Even horses are not immune, as it has been said that they will shy and slip if brought to the ring.

A dewpond has long been associated with Chanctonbury, although not always the same one. From 1874 it was famed as the largest in Sussex, but during the Second World War it disappeared, and has since been replaced by a modern substitute.

When you become sated with all the mysteries of the ring, you may

The Ring minus most of its familiar crown of trees following the Great Storm of October 16, 1987

descend by a choice of tracks including one with the lovely name of Heaven's Gate.

Lastly a weather proverb speaks of Lady Goring's Nightcap. The rhyme goes:

> *Old Mother Goring's got her cap on,*
> *so we shall soon have some wet.*

This refers to the mist which descends on the top of the Ring on certain days, warning of rain to follow.

CHARITIES

OUR ancestors seemed to have found much time to think about the hereafter and what would happen after their own demise. Leaving a sum of money to provide a dole or charity for those in need was a certain way of ensuring that your name lived on, and perhaps your own soul would benefit in the process. Some of these ancient charities have lapsed or have been changed, but happily some still live on.

At Henfield Dame Elizabeth Gresham (a member of the local Byshopp family) died more than 300 years ago, leaving a field of seven acres (another was added later), to provide rent to be distributed annually on All Hallows Day (November 1). The first ten shillings went to a minister to preach a sermon, and the rest to clothe poor people. On her memorial was written: 'Her piety, prudence, equanimity and charity outlive her person', although the writer may not have realised that her charity would be remembered so many years later. Originally the bequest must have been distributed in the church, but in more modern times it was carried on in the Old Coffee Tavern, or the Assembly Rooms. Subsequently the practice of distributing the charity in church was resumed.

In addition to Dame Gresham's Charity, Henfield once had two others, Thomas Canon's Charity and the Beggarman's Bequest, but these have both been extinct for a number of years.

At Hartfield there is the Nicholas Smith Charity, which is distributed annually on Good Friday, by his grave, to the poor of the parish. The story behind this bequest has all the stamp of a folk legend. Apparently Nicholas Smith (said to be known as Dog Smith) was a fairly rich man who decided to test the kindness of his countrymen by travelling around dressed as a tramp. He was disappointed in his reception at most places in Sussex, until he got to Hartfield. So it was here that he settled, and upon his death left the annual bequest.

At little Piddinghoe, Edith Croft died aged three months in 1868. Her grandmother was determined that her short life should not be forgotten, and she founded a charity to be known as Little Edith's Treat, with money to be spent on July 19 each year – Edith's birthday. As the name implies the bequest is in the form of a treat for the village children.

Henfield, home of several charities, pictured c1920

There are many more of these interesting charities, but one more must suffice. In his book *The Wonderful Weald* (1911), Arthur Beckett wrote about a certain East Hoathly parson whose ragged style of dress offended one particular lady of his congregation. To show her feelings in the matter, the lady promised to give him a new pair of breeches annually, and what is more she is supposed to have presented his successors with a piece of woodland from which an income could be devoted to the renewal of the current parson's breeches. Beckett said that the wood still existed and was known as Breeches Wood. However when I enquired of the charity from a modern day rector, he confessed to have no knowledge of the charity.

CHILDREN'S GAMES

THIS is truly a vast subject, and one which completely ignores county boundaries. All I can do in a book of this sort is to offer a sampling of the riches that are available.

Hoops have virtually disappeared as children's playthings, but in my mother's childhood at the turn of the century, they were highly prized. The boys had metal hoops, depending on the local blacksmith to provide these and to keep them in running order. They were driven by a piece of metal known as a skidder, a skiddaw, a skellaer, a skeeler or perhaps a skimmer – depending on which village you came from. The girls used wooden hoops, considerably lighter than the boys'. My mother looked upon hers as a child nowadays might prize a cycle, running for miles with her hoop without apparent tiredness. Alfred Ridel, in *Ninfield in the Nineties* (1979), gives us an insight into the importance that the owners placed on their hoops, as iron bolts or hooks were provided on the outside of the school for 'parking'. An innovation was a cotton reel revolving on a nail fixed at an angle near the end of the skidder. Mr Goatcher of Washington told me of how gangs of boys with their hoops would charge each other from opposite ends of the road, attempting to knock over as many of the other's hoops as possible (and presumably often their owners with them).

As popular as hoops were tops, which were of various kinds. Mr Laker of Three Bridges recalled how the boys would play with their tops before school, and when the bell rang would hurriedly run into the building, often leaving their tops and string in the road. Mrs Rapley who kept a small shop near the school, and who was noted for her mean nature, would gather up the tops and the strings – scrubbing the tops and re-selling them in her shop, and even winding up the strings into halfpenny balls.

Knucklebones were a favourite of my mother. These were sets of stones of an equal roundness, with which a clever child could perform all manner of tricks, such as placing five of the stones on the back of the hand, and throwing the remaining one in the air. Before you caught it again, you had to remove one of the others. Another trick was to put one stone in your mouth, throwing up the remainder, and removing the stone from your mouth before you caught the others. Other permutations were endless.

Kiss in the Ring seems to have been particularly popular in Sussex, and not merely as a children's game. At Hove it was said to result in a good deal of wild behaviour, so much so that in 1897 the *Brighton Herald* was happy to report 'Kiss in the Ring was only indulged in by a limited number, and it was of a decidedly mild order'.

Of the vast number of outdoor games, here is an unusual one recalled by SL Longhurst of Battle in 1979. It was called bully-rooten (or something similar) and was played with spars (hazel sticks used in thatching). Each player in turn raises a spar over his shoulder, and swings it so that the sharp end beds into the soft earth. The next player does the same with his spar, at an angle across the previous one, endeavouring to uproot it. Each player follows, and any uprooted in this way is out. The others continue until only one, the winner, is left. This was a game popular in autumn or spring in the stackyards where the ground was moist.

Many will have memories of playground singing games. In 1957 I persuaded a Sussex newspaper to conduct an enquiry into children's singing games popular at that time. Many lists were contributed, the longest being of forty-four games, although this list seemed to have been padded out with nursery rhymes. None appeared to have a definite Sussex connection, but several of the rhymes which accompanied the games were remembered by my mother from her childhood half a century earlier.

Whilst the girls played their singing games, the boys were more likely indulging in something like British bulldog, which several people have told me was always popular in Sussex. In this there were two teams opposite each other, in single file. The front boys folded their arms and hopped towards their opposite number, attempting to knock him off balance. The side with most members left hopping, were the winners.

Some games were particularly popular at specific times of the year. On Boxing Day, oranges were rolled along the streets, the object being to hit the fruit belonging to another. If successful, then the orange was forfeited (this was noted at Brighton in 1883). During the summer, schoolchildren rolled round cheeses down a steep hill at Forest Row (noted in 1894).

To conclude this very brief look at a big subject, here is a party game contributed in 1988 by D Lewry of Newhaven, from his youth. A pudding basin is filled with flour, and a plate placed over it, so that

Children at play, St Nicholas School, Portslade, c1910

it may be safely inverted. The basin is then removed, leaving a 'pudding' of flour on the plate. A ring, such as a plain gold wedding ring, is then gently dropped on to the top of the flour. Each player is issued with a playing card and in turn has to cut a slice off the pudding, without disturbing the ring. The unfortunate who causes the ring to fall has to fetch it out of the flour with his (or her) nose.

CHILDREN'S RHYMES

AS well as rhymes associated with singing games, there were also many concerned with all kinds of other things. For instance school and home, both places where children learnt early on to behave or face the consequences – as in this terse rhyme:

> *Love is one thing,*
> *Father's belts another.*
> *If you don't get one,*
> *You're sure to get the other.*

But not all rhymes were so threatening. Many concerned natural things:

> *The first butterfly you see,*
> *Cut off it's head across your knee,*
> *Bury the head under a stone,*
> *And a lot of money you will own.*

Or this one concerned with lady bugs (ladybirds):

> *Bishop, Bishop Barnabee,*
> *Tell me when my wedding shall be.*
> *If it be tomorrow day,*
> *Open your wings and fly away.*

Food was always a popular subject:

> *Pea pod hucks, twenty for a pin.*
> *If you doant like em, I'll take em back agin.*

White specks on the nails were supposed to indicate gifts:

> *A gift on the thumb, is sure to come.*
> *A gift on the finger, is sure to linger.*

Many rhymes poked fun at the establishment, such as this skit on a hymn beloved of teetotalers:

Dare to be Daniel,
Dare to stand alone,
Dare to pass a public house,
And take the money home.

Local 'characters' were always good subjects for rhyme, as this from Forest Row:

Old Miss Parker, with her dainty feet,
Makes her way along a muddy street.

Or this one from Portslade, remembered by Ethel Powell:

Here's Granny Rumney, on her pattens.
Fast as she goes, her tongue goes clacken.

Pattens were worn instead of boots when the weather was wet. Winifred Cousins remembered them as flat pieces of thick wood, shaped to the foot, and fastened with a lace.

There is one rhyme which although it always deals with a particular teacher, crops up all over Sussex: Here is the version remembered by Ted Roberts from his days at Sussex Road School, Worthing (now the Sydney Walter Centre):

Mr Dicks is a very nice man,
He tries to teach you all he can,
Readin', writin', rithmetic.
But he never forgets to give you the stick.
When he does he makes you dance,
Out of England, into France.
Out of France and into Spain,
Over the hills and back again.

From nearby Findon, this is how their version went:

Miss Bull teaches the school.
Readin', writin', and arithmetic.
And she doesn't forget to give you the stick.
When she does she makes you dance,

Over from England, into France.
From France and into Spain,
Over the hills and back again.

A version from Petworth has the teacher named as Mr Brown, but with the rest of the rhyme similar to the Worthing one.

In *Kirdford – The Old Parish Rediscovered,* by Janet Austin (1990) there is a much longer example, where the school teacher is Old Daddy Goodacre. The first part is similar to the ones already quoted, but it then goes on to tell you that the teacher was a Lancashire man, 'Where everything is better' and ends with the line: 'We wish he would go back there as soon as he can.'

Apparently Mr Goodacre heard some of his pupils chanting this song, and handed out 'six of the best'. It seems he regularly sent the boys out to cut caning sticks from the hedges.

When children escaped from school, they could start their working lives by becoming bird scarers on one of the local farms. This was one of their rhymes:

We've ploughed the land,
We've sowed the seed,
We've made all neat and gay,
So take a bit, and leave a bit,
Away, birds, away.

Lastly here are some rhymes found in a child's autograph album from the 1920s:

Steal not this book, for fear of shame.
For in it is the owner's name.
And when you're dead the Lord will say,
Where is that book you stole away?

This was typical of the inscriptions found at the front of many books owned by children. The advertisements for Beecham's Pills ('worth a guinea a box') made a deep impression on young minds — with rhymes like this.

Hark the Herald Angels sing,
Beecham's Pills are very good things.
Peace on earth and mercy mild,
One for a woman and two for a child.

Surely the last line is the wrong way round?
Or perhaps:

Mary had a little watch.
She swallowed it one day.
And now she's taking Beecham's Pills,
To pass the time away.

But not all were rude. Many who wrote in the books were anxious to claim to be the very last. For instance:

By hook or by crook, I'll be last in this book.

But the endpaper was then used for the following:

By pen or by paint, I'll see that you aint.

Or to really have the final word:

To diddle another, I'll write on the cover.

Another picture of the children of St Nicholas School, c1911

CHRISTMAS

PREPARATIONS for Christmas started in Sussex with Stir-up Sunday (the last Sunday before Advent, when the Collect of the Mass begins 'Stir up we beseech thee, O Lord'). The Sussex housewives took this to mean that they should make their Christmas puddings in readiness for the festivities. All the family had a hand in the ritual stirring, making a wish which, of course had to be kept secret. The spoon was of wood (as was the manger at Bethlehem), and it had to be moved clockwise (the way the Three Wise Men travelled). Failure of any parts of the ritual would bring bad luck. At Brighton children chanted:

> Stir up we beseech three, the pudding in the pot.
> And when we get home, we'll eat it all hot.

Christmas puddings in their present form are a modern creation. In the past it was plumm pottage or plum broth, a mixture of sweet and savoury, eaten at the start of the Christmas meal. Timothy Burrell of Cuckfield noted in his diary in 1706 that his Christmas meal began with plumm pottage, but it also reappeared later on in the proceedings.

The pleasant custom of putting coins or charms in Christmas puddings came in during the nineteenth century. In 1840 Queen Victoria ordered that gold sovereigns be placed in her puddings. When charms were used, each one had its own particular significance – a silver thimble meant that the finder would stay single, a bell or ring meant a wedding, and horseshoes stood for good luck

December 21 (St Thomas's Day and the shortest day of the year) was considered particularly good for any kind of divination. If a girl wished to dream of her lover on this night, she placed a peeled onion in a handkerchief under her pillow, reciting:

> Good St Thomas do me right
> And see my true love comes tonight.
> In the clothes and in the array,
> That he weareth every day.

December 21 was also the day when the yule log was brought into the house, to burn if possible until Twelfth Night. This day was also known as Gooding Day (*ibid*).

Christmas Day itself seems to have been observed quietly in most Sussex homes, perhaps the greatest excitement being provided by the Christmas mummers (or, in Sussex, tipteers)(*ibid*).

Food was always important. Mince pies were once made with real meat, and in Sussex were traditionally shaped like the manger. As recently as 1944 a woman in Newhaven commented 'It isn't Christian' when her daughter presented her with a round mince pie. Each pie made

The traditional Christmas kissing bough, once often seen in Sussex

by a different cook represented a happy month. Mothers with daughters in service (as most had in days gone by) would send boxes of pies by the carrier, telling them to be sure and make a wish when eating the first one. The ingredients were supposed to include some smuggled brandy for extra flavour, and a little powdered rosemary, based on the legend that Mary hung the Christ Child's clothes on a rosemary bush to dry.

It was considered lucky to keep Christmas cakes a year before consuming them, and it was also lucky to eat gingerbread on Christmas Day.

Before Turkeys were the favourite Christmas meat in Sussex, it would have been the Christmas goose. Children chanted:

> *Christmas is coming, the goose is gettin' fat.*
> *Please put a penny in the old man's hat.*

If was also believed that if the goose bone were thick, then the winter weather would be severe.

The wassail bowl contained spiced wine or ale, with nutmeg, sugar and ginger. This was often referred to as lamb's wool and was said to be very popular with Sussex shepherds.

Children went from door to door with a doll in a cradle, representing the Christ Child, and sang:

We wish you a merry Christmas and a Happy New Year,
A pocket full of money and a barrel full of beer.

On Boxing Day, or anytime up to Twelfth Night, the howlers took the place of the mummers, wassailing the apple trees (*ibid*).

While on the subject of apples, here is a game coupled with a superstition, which was played on Christmas night in Sussex.

Apples were fastened on a string which was hung and twirled before the open fire. The owner of the apple which fell first was said to be ready to get married. As they fell so the order of marriage for the rest was indicated. The owner of the last apple to fall would remain single.

Father Christmas from the Ruper Mummers Play

CHURCH IN THE WOOD

THE little medieval church at Hollington, near Hastings, is one of several in Sussex which were supposed to have been built some distance away from the intended site, due to interference by the Devil, or some other evil spirits. The Hollington legend was printed thus in the 1845 edition of *A Handbook for Hastings* by W Diplock.

'A church being commenced at a short distance, the builders every morning when they came to their work, found all their labours of the preceding day utterly demolished, and the very materials also vanished. This sorely puzzled them, til at last one day a countryman happening to pass through an unfrequented wood, found there, to his no small surprise, a church newly built; the Evil One having contrived, since he could not entirely prevent the erection of the church, to get it placed where no-one could easily approach it'.

The often quoted explanation of this sort of legend is that the builders of early churches in Sussex were troubled by those who resented the 'new religion', and difficulties were placed in their way, when they tried to build on what were traditionally non-Christian sites.

When Hollington Church really was surrounded by trees, it captured the imagination of nineteenth century writers, such as Charles Lamb, who described it as 'a little churchling in the midst of a wood that seems dropped by an angel that was tired of carrying two packages'.

One further item of folklore concerning the church is that it was said by many to have been the church were the two lovers from Fairlight were married. (See Lovers Seat).

The Church in the Wood

CHURCH MARKS

Cowfold Church, where church marks survive

A NUMBER of Sussex churchyards had names of farms in the parish inscribed on their wooden fences, indicating the owners' share in the cost of repairs required. Among the churchyards which had these marks were Ardingly, Berwick, Chiddingly, Edburton, Henfield, Herstmonceux, Itchingfield, Kirdford, Lindfield, Rusper, Sedlescombe, West Hoathly and Woodmancote. Few of the marks survive, although they may still be seen at Cowfold, where they date back to at least the seventeenth century; thirty-five names existed in 1682.

In the eighteenth century many of the wooden churchyard fences were replaced with stone or brick walls, so the custom became much less widespread.

CISSBURY RING

ALTHOUGH historically very important, from a purely folklore aspect Cissbury does not rate as highly as Chanctonbury. Most people will most readily think of the Stone Age flint mines when Cissbury Ring is mentioned. These were as deep as fifty feet, with tunnels similar to modern-day coal mines, except that the people who toiled in them had to make use of the most primitive tools. In 1867 a woman was found buried upside-down in a vertical position, with no indication of why. However no legends seem to have attached themselves to such a find.

The best known folk story associated with Cissbury is of a tunnel said to have been discovered in the 1860s, leading from Offington Hall (now demolished), to the Ring (more than two miles away). The tunnel was found behind panelling in the library, leading via the cellars to a vast treasure. The owner of the Hall was said to have offered half of the proceeds to anyone who could clear the passage and obtain the spoils. However the treasure was guarded by large snakes that attacked anyone who disturbed them, and none of the treasure seekers was successful.

Another legend connected with the Cissbury area is of a phantom highwayman, who was sentenced to death following capture, and was buried in a grave excavated in the middle of the road where some of his crimes had been committed. He is supposed to have vowed that he would never remain in his grave, and it was said that after his burial, his body was found on top of the grave. Several more attempts to inter him ended in the same fashion. Presumably he eventually stayed put, although his ghost then haunted the roadway. One story was of a coach held up by a highwaymen, with the driver attempting to run the thief down. He was shocked to find his horses passing through the mounted man. Carters also claimed that they 'bumped' over something solid at a particular spot, although nothing was ever seen.

Cissbury Ring was once known as Old Bury or The Bury. As recently as the nineteenth century revels were held there, with the game of Kiss in the Ring very popular with the young people. They danced in a ring singing 'Hey-diddle-derry, let's dance on The Bury'. When these goings-on became a bit too free and easy older and wiser heads decided that they should be stopped.

CORPUS CHRISTI

ENGLAND of pre-reformation times returns each year to Arundel on the feast of Corpus Christi, when the Sacred Host is carried in procession from the Roman Catholic cathedral, to the quadrangle of Arundel Castle. In ancient times it was customary to strew flowers in the path of important people, and so this custom was adopted by the church when the Blessed Sacrament was to be carried in procession. In many European countries the custom is still widespread, and Arundel's annual observance was borrowed from the village of Sutri, near Rome, by the fifteenth Duke of Norfolk, in 1877.

The flowers are woven by a dedicated band of women into a glorious carpet, which stretches down the whole of the length of the cathedral. Many thousands come to view the carpet, before it is walked upon by the Bishop and priests, as the procession begins its way to the castle grounds. The Sacred Host in its golden monstrance is carried by the Bishop, and becomes the focal point of the ceremony.

There was a break during World War One but the custom has continued ever since, and is now one of the largest processions of this kind in the country. The fine cathedral was opened in 1873, with the original dedication to St Philip Neri. In 1976 it was rededicated to Our Lady and St Philip Howard.

The carpet of flowers in the cathedral at Arundel, c1930

THE CRAWLEY ELM

The elm pictured early in the twentieth century

ONCE a local landmark on The Green at Crawley, the old elm tree was traditionally believed to be 800 years old. Known as The Doctor's Tree, it was near to the home of Dr Robert Smith, who in the 1790s was a popular local personality. In its prime the tree could have been about 140 feet high, but by 1824 it was in partial ruins, with an estimated height of twenty-two feet. The hollow centre had a gothic doorway leading into a brick-floored chamber. By 1860 it was down to fifteen feet, although the door still remained, and there was a fence around it. The interior was said to be large enough to hold a dozen people, but after a tramp spent a night there and set light to the tree, the door had to be kept locked.

In 1883 part of the tree was carried away by a storm, and by 1914 The door had disappeared. By this time it was only 10 feet high, although still alive. Crawley children once had their awkward questions answered by being told that they came from The Doctor's Tree. During its long life it had been used as a hostel, a billet for soldiers, and for tea parties and local meetings. In the mid 1930s it was said to have been demolished as unsafe, although according to

Crawley early in the twentieth century

local memories even then some part of it survived.

The tree featured in Conan Doyle's Sussex novel *Rodney Stone,* and a Madame de Genlis who visited Crawley in 1823 was sufficiently impressed by the tree to write about it in the *London Literary Gazette* of May 24, 1823. She reported that the inhabitants met there to enjoy their pipes and tell old tales.

Much local folklore surrounded the tree. A wayfarer was supposed to have given birth to a child there, the parish beadle is said to have used it as a lock-up and the local children assembled at the tree for their annual march to the Rectory for Easter hot cross buns and prizes.

CUCKOO LORE

THE cuckoo is probably the bird which crops up most often in Sussex folklore. There are many superstitions, plus rhymes, phrases and songs. Here are just a few of them.

On hearing the first cuckoo you should turn your money over in your pocket, in order to double it. To hear it on an empty stomach means death or sorrow. To hear it in bed is likewise very unlucky, but it is considered lucky to remove your right sock or stocking reciting at the same time 'May this to me, be lucky be'. If you are unfortunate enough to suffer with lumbago, then this can be relieved by rolling on the ground at the first call. Another good idea was to look under your right foot, where you should find a hair of the colour of the person you will marry.

Babies born on the day of the first cuckoo's call were said to be particularly lucky throughout their life. Sussex labourers enjoyed the cuckoo's arrival, as at the sound of the first 'cuck' they took themselves off to the nearest hostelry to drink the bird's health in 'cuckoo ale'.

Other strange cuckoo beliefs included the notion that the ashes of a roasted bird would relieve stomach pains, fits and malaria. But as it was considered very unlucky to bring the bird into the house, we are not told how one would manage to procure the roasted ashes. A dry spell of weather was said to be 'the cuckoo clearing away the mud'. persistent cuckoo calls are said to forecast rainy weather, and girls waiting to be wed would work out how long this would be by counting the calls. Two for two years' wait, three for three and so on.

There were many cuckoo rhymes. This one varies slightly as recalled by different people; this was how my mother remembered it:

> *In April come he will.*
> *In May sings all day.*
> *In June he changes his tune.*
> *In July he prepares to fly.*
> *In August go he must.*
> *If he stays until September,*
> *Tis as much as the oldest man can remember.*

Another jingle went as follows:

When the cuckoo comes to the bare thorn,
Sell your cow and buy your corn.
But when she comes to the full bit.
Sell your corn and buy your sheep.

Similar sentiments were expressed in the shorter rhyme:

Bad for the barley and good for the corn.
When the cuckoo comes to an empty thorn.

The following song was very well known in Sussex. Many older folk will remember singing in the schoolroom:

The cuckoo is a pretty bird, she singeth as she flies.
She bringeth us good tidings, and telleth us no lies.
She sucks the birds eggs, to make her voice clear.
And when she singeth cuckoo, the summer draweth near.

There are many slight variations to the above words, but they usually end something like this:

The cuckoo comes in April, she sings a song in May.
In June she beats upon the drum, and then she flies away.

Sometimes the above lines become part of different songs, becoming what are known as 'floating' verses.

Heathfield is the place most commonly associated with the cuckoo – older folk will know the village as 'Heffle'. The most often quoted legend is that the first cuckoo is released from a basket (or poke) by an old gypsy woman (or witch) on April 14. She has charge of all the cuckoos, which she takes to Heathfield Fair, releasing them as the fancy takes her. This particular fair is said to date from the fourteenth century, and the belief in the cuckoo woman appears to go back a very long way, although no one can say how it originated. In 1868 a Fittleworth woman complained that the cuckoo-keeper was very bad tempered that year, and had let only one bird out of her basket and 'that 'ere bird is nothin' to call a singer'.

High Street, Heathfield, home of Heffle Fair, in the 1920s

The use of the word cuckoo is common in the county. There are cuckoo gates (more often called kissing gates), cuckoo bread and cheese (children's name for the hawthorn when in bud); cuckoo in the nest and cuckoo as a term applied to a stupid person (gowk was also another name for both a cuckoo and a fool). There were many plant names which made use of the word cuckoo – cuckoo grass, cuckoo pint, cuckoo dye, cuckoo's stocking, and several others.

CURSES

CURSE, the very word makes the fainthearted shiver, and even the brave feel a bit uneasy. No doubt many of the curses uttered in Sussex in the past were the last resort of someone driven to despair, but tradition could be relied on to come up with a suitably horrific result, even if this was difficult to prove.

Consider poor William de Braose whose wife and son had been starved to death in Bramber Castle by King John. William knew that the Bramber woods were a favourite hunting place of John, so he uttered these dramatic words: 'I call upon the damned to likewise damn the Bramber Woods of Sussex, and may John and his creed ne'er walk in peace'.

Probably the best known Sussex curse was the one said to have been invoked by the departing monks of Battle Abbey, when Sir Anthony Browne was given their property by Henry VIII. The church had the right words for such a curse, beginning with: 'By the authority of almighty God and Blessed Peter, Prince of the apostles, to whom it is committed by God the power to bind and loose on earth, let vengeance be declared on the malefactors, robbers and spoliators of the goods and possessions, rights and liberties, of the monastery. . .' and much more in similar vein. The nub of the curse was that 'by fire and water thy line shall come to an end'. The curse seems to have worked, although it took more than 250 years to do so.

It was in 1793 that the great house of Cowdray, owned by Sir Anthony's heirs, was gutted by fire and all its treasures destroyed. At about the same time the eighth and last Lord Montague was drowned in an attempt to negotiate the falls at Schaffhausen on the Rhine. The property then passed to his sister, who bore two sons and three daughters. Her husband, out in a boat with the two boys in 1815, had a mishap, and the sons were both drowned. As far back at 1851 a curate at Easebourne wrote that he frequently heard the locals talking about the curse, so the tale has endured for quite a long while.

A legend of Frant church tells how, during extensive alterations in 1858, the grave of a young woman who had been buried in her bridal gown was accidentally damaged. A local story said that a curse had been placed on anyone who disturbed her; accordingly three people who had been involved in the excavations died within the year.

A somewhat similar tale, this time from South Heighton, tells of how in the early part of this century, a farmer ignored warnings of a curse on anyone who cut down a line of ancient trees. But this was done, and it was said that his farm became haunted by 'a strange presence'.

Sometimes curses are really the result of local people's dislike of change. Bognor vicars were said to have lived under a curse, when the old St John's Chapel in the Steyne was demolished, leaving just the tower. To make matters worse, the material was sold to a builder for non-ecclesiastical use. However the subsequent demolition of the later St John's Church in 1972 was thought to have brought the curse to an end.

While in the same area, a Felpham curse was written about by Gerard Young in his book *The Cottage in the Fields* (1945). An old cottage stood on church property and the vicar wanted it removed. The demolition men arrived when the family were at dinner, and the distraught mother looked at the cleric and said quietly, 'One above will remember you for this'. Years later the family moved back to Felpham, and one day the mother saw the old vicar being helped along the road, a victim of a form of paralysis. She looked at him as they passed and said, 'God did not forget you'.

Sussex is rich in similar stories, but to end, here is one told to me in quite recent times by a local woman. It concerns Broadbridge Heath, near Horsham, where an important local landowner caught a gypsy boy on the Common, throwing stones at birds. He thrashed the boy with his horse whip, beating him to death. The boy's mother cursed him, declaring that the male line of his family would not continue, and this proved correct.

THE DEVIL

SUSSEX folk have a strange attitude where the Prince of Darkness is concerned. They hold him in a slightly tolerant, almost affectionate regard; secure in the knowledge that he cannot really harm them, and that any Sussex man is more than a match for anything that Satan can throw at him.

Even the Sussex howlers' (mummers') version of the Devil. in the guise of Beelzebub, turns out to be slightly more humourous than evil.

> *In my hand a frying pan,*
> *Don't you think I'm a funny old man.*

The Devil has many alternative names in Sussex – indeed there seems no end to the ingenuity of the Sussex countryman in avoiding the use of the obvious, when speaking about Satan. Thus we have Mr Grimm, Old Nick, The Old Man, The Poor Man or just He. I have even heard him spoken of as Old Lawrence, but perhaps this had a particularly local connection. However, the Devil appears as such in many Sussex names of places; for instance the best known of all – Devil's Dyke. Then there are names of natural features like the Devil's Punchbowl on the Downs, The Devil's Footprints, The Devil's Jumps (barrows), and the Devil's (and his wife's) Grave.

The first of an old set of pictures telling the
story in rhyme of Devil's Dyke

The best known piece of the Devil's work in Sussex
– Devil's Dyke, near Poynings

Superstitions and legends abound. At the Devil's Dyke the Evil One tried to drown all the little Christian churches in Sussex, and was thwarted by an old woman, helped in many versions by St Cuthman. At Mayfield he appeared to St Dunstan, but as usual was easily outwitted when the Saint spotted his tell-tale cloven feet beneath the gown of an apparently attractive female visitor. In St Leonard's Forest the Devil challenged a smuggler to a race, but lost and the smuggler, Mick Miles, retained his soul. The number seven seems to have a particular attraction for the Devil. Run round Chanctonbury Ring seven times to see the Evil One on Midsummer Eve; run round the Devil's Humps at Stoughton, and he will appear. Walk round Northiam Unitarian Chapel seven times on Midsummer Eve, and you will see his Satanic Majesty.

In Sussex dialect and word-lore the Devil crops up repeatedly. Magpies are the Devil's children. Many Devil's Lanes exist throughout the county. The *Devil's dancing hour* is very early in the morning. To *beat the Devil round the gooseberry bush* is when a speaker inflicts a long rigmarole on his audience. *As black as the*

Devil's nutting bag is exceedingly black. *The Devil's own luck* means exactly what it says. *To hold the candle to the Devil, although you begrudge him the light,* means to grudgingly give in to someone. *When the Devil was ill, the Devil a saint could be. When the Devil was well, the Devil a saint was he.* Satan's Snuff Boxes were toadstools on the Down. Lastly (and this section of the book could go on and on) here are a few old beliefs associated with Mr Grimm. On October 10 the Devil spits on the blackberries, making them not worth picking. The Devil tried to destroy the blue scabious on the Downs, because of its healing powers. When eating boiled eggs you should always break the bottom of the eggs, or the Devil will use them as boats. This has been attributed to the Brighton fishermen, but it seems to be much more widespread. Go nutting on a Sunday, and the Devil will hold down the branches for you. Horse brasses in the house will catch the Devil's attention, and distract him away from more serious mischief. And remember that if you cut your nails on a Sunday, then the Devil will chase you all the following week.

Even in his own particular domain he seems to have had little luck. In the song *The Farmer's Curst Wife* (also known as *The Sussex Whistling Song* because of the whistling chorus) the Devil accepts a farmer's wife and carries her down to Hell. But there she makes his life a misery, and he quickly returns her to her unwilling husband.

DOWSING

FEW people would dispute the gift of divining or dowsing, although there are aspects of it that properly fall into the field of folklore. Why can some folk get results where others fail, and can the gift be handed on in families? Even more intriguingly, why is it said to work on maps and pictures, and with many kinds of objects besides water.

The usual method is to employ a Y-shaped hazel stick, held by its two prongs, with the other end resolutely turning upwards when water is found. There are however many variations. Some appear to have the gift well established, whilst others have it in a much lesser degree. There are many obvious advantages for some other trades, such as well-diggers.

George Roberts, water diviner of Henfield

Rudyard Kipling, when he lived at Batemans in Burwash, used a water diviner to decide where his well should be sunk. Kipling was a hands-on man, and was interested enough to grip one of the two prongs of the hazel fork. He wrote: 'When we stopped at twenty-five feet, we had found a Jacobean tobacco pipe, a Cromwellian laten spoon, and part of a Roman horse bit'.

Mr Goatcher, a retired market gardener of Washington, explained to me how his well had been dug. Originally the builder had proposed to sink a well near the back door of the house. But Mr Godman, a local dowser, pronounced that there was no water at all near the back door. He did however find a spring some distance away and said that water would be found there about twenty-five feet down. This proved to be perfectly true, and during the time the well was in use it never failed to produce all the clear water that was needed, although other village wells, four times as deep, ran dry. The water had a very fine taste. When Mr Goatcher tried his hand with the hazel twig nothing happened, but when Mr Godman gripped his hand, the twig leapt at the correct spot.

Bill Muddle, who when younger lived at Henfield, told me a great deal about the a locally famous water diviner George Roberts, who before World War One had an undertakers and builders business. George had perfected his dowsing to a fine art, and had become an authority on the subject, travelling through the Sussex, Kent, Surrey and Hampshire, finding water where others had failed. Mr Muddle said he could never understand how it worked for George Roberts, and yet he himself was unable to get any results, although using the same technique. Mr Roberts even had his own trade cards printed, with a picture of himself employing his gift.

A lady at a Wisborough Green talk told me that her mother had been the local dowser in the village. She used the customary hazel stick, and found her results so strong that she could not prevent the twig moving, even when she tried. Part of her gift was to be able to tell where the deepest water was to be found. The daughter had tried to follow her mother's success, but without any results whatever.

The Virgin Mary Spring at Petworth, 1904

DRAGONS

REPORTS of dragons and large snakes go back a long way in Sussex. Lillian Candlin, the folklorist, wondered if the tales could be due to the survival in Sussex of the komodo dragon, the largest lizard in the world. There is always the possibility that dragons could be a folk memory of long extinct prehistoric creatures such as dinosaurs. Many traces of such animals have been discovered in the county, at places as far apart as Billingshurst, Southwater, Crawley, Warnham, Hastings, Battle and Crowhurst. We are speaking of several million years ago, but the folk-process can still surprise us with its extreme tenacity.

The best known Sussex dragon legends are connected with St. Leonard's Forest, near Horsham, and these will be dealt with later under the name of the saint. The next best known Sussex dragon was at Lyminster, where the animal was known as the knucker.

Several knucker holes are found at different Sussex locations, including Lancing, Shoreham, Worthing and Angmering, as well as the famous one at Lyminster. These holes were thought to be bottomless pools, and several local stories exist telling how villagers joined the church bell ropes together to try and plumb the depths, but always without success. The knucker of Lyminster figures in a very persistent legend, and as is usual in such tales the culmination is in the slaying of the dragon, of which there are several different versions. Some will tell you that it was the King of Sussex who offered his daughter's hand in marriage to anyone brave enough to slay the knucker. A wandering knight succeeded and lived happily with his princess for the rest of their lives. The better known version tells of a local boy, Jim Puttock (or some such similar name), who baked a huge pudding which he offered to the dragon. It stuck in the creature's throat and the villagers helped to kill the beast, and chop it into pieces. A correspondent in a newspaper in 1965 compared this method with one used in East Africa to kill crocodiles. Sometimes the pudding becomes a pie, and it was young Jim who single-handed cut off the knucker's head. No one should doubt the story, as Jim's tombstone can still be seen at the church, with a worn design of a cross upon a herring-bone pattern background.

As a young boy Bill Lindfield of Sompting heard stories of what he thought were 'nigger holes'. Later he realised that they were actually

Near Cissbury Ring

referring to knucker holes. He was told of a hole at Brooklands which had been tested for depth with the church bell ropes, but even they did not reach the bottom. When the Sussex Pad inn at Shoreham was on fire, the firemen put their hoses into one of these holes, but when they had finished it was noted that the level of the water had not fallen. The knucker hole at Lyminster may still be seen, although it is very inaccessible.

At Cissbury Ring a tunnel was guarded, legend says, by a 'nest of dragons'. Then there was the dragon that lived near Bignor Hill, with the marks of its coils to be seen on the side of the hill. Sussex author Esther Meynell wrote of a dragon lying asleep in the waters of Swanbourne Lake, although she seems the only writer to have noted it

Sussex people have always thought that dragons and snakes brought ill luck – no doubt the Christian allegorical tales had something to do with this belief.

EFFIGIES

THE construction of a recognisable effigy of a local man or woman was, for many years, a means of showing disapproval of their way of life, or of some particular action. For instance child -or wife-beating might lead to the perpetrators being singled out in this way, often accompanied by 'rough music' (*ibid*) after dark. Shrovetide was the season most noted for effigies, when unpopular local figures found themselves held up to ridicule, to be pelted with stones and brickbats. Bonfire Night was another time when effigies in the shape of guys might be based on hated figures. In 1859 an un-named clergyman was the subject for a huge effigy, following his adoption of high-church liturgy.

At Lewes, effigies of Pope Paul V, Guy Fawkes and of dubious national and international figures are carried in procession before being consigned to the bonfire – along with effigies of 'enemies of bonfire' – local politicians and townsfolk who have attracted odium.

Other figures favoured by the mob included General Booth of the Salvation Army, as well as dishonest traders, law officers, and many

The Bishopric, Horsham, in Henry Burstow's day, and the place where the effigy was hung on the inn sign

An effigy of Pope Paul V carried in procession through Lewes streets on Bonfire Night

national personalities.

St Crispin's Day in Horsham (October 25) was celebrated by the shoemakers, who regarded this saint as their own. Henry Burstow, in his *Reminiscences of Horsham* (1911), said that the townsfolk were interested in the day as it was the occasion for holding up to ridicule anyone who had become particularly notorious during the preceding year. An effigy of each offender (sometimes there were two together) was hung on the signpost of one of the public houses near to their home. There it stayed until November 5 when it would be taken down and burned. Before the day people would be conjecturing who would be the 'Crispin'. One year the effigies of a man and his wife who had ill-treated a boy were hung on the sign of the Green Dragon in the Bishopric. On November 5 a hostile group went to their house, and smashed the man's handcart. For this the mob were fined £2 each, although this was quickly made up by public donations.

Effigies of unpopular figures have not entirely disappeared in modern times. In the 1980s, at a pub in Guestling, a figure intended to represent Ebenezer Ramsey, who had been the publican in 1888, and who had committed suicide by hanging himself in the inn's stables, was pelted with coins by the locals, the money going to local charities.

EMPIRE DAY

MAY 24, Queen Victoria's birthday, was celebrated during the inter-war years as Empire Day - taking over very largely the place of the traditional May Day (May 1) in many schools' calendars. It appeared to be welcomed by authority, who had to some extent looked upon May Day as the remains of a pagan festival. School teachers were not quite sure whether to encourage the making of May garlands by their pupils, by giving them a whole or half holiday, or to attempt to ignore the whole thing. Empire Day was considered completely 'safe', and so was welcomed by schools with enthusiasm and given the stamp of official approval.

In spite of all the patriotic fervour, which included songs, children dressed in costumes of the empire, cheers for Queen Victoria, and much flag-waving, some of the old May Day customs still lingered, or became mixed with the Empire Day jingoism. Children danced around the Maypole with flowers in their hair, and although the ribbon-plaiting dances were not exactly traditionally English, they still appeared a little more genuine than the 'hurrahs' and red and white paper flowers.

Empire Day, Lewes 1908

A Masque of Empire on Empire Day at Rudgwick, 1909

But although Empire Day has disappeared, to be supplanted by Commonwealth Day (with little to single it out from any other day of the year), we must not overlook the fervour with which it was celebrated for around fifty years. For instance Mrs Laughton of Horsham used to sit a a table outside her house in Brighton Road, giving out threepenny joeys to all the schoolchildren. Now that really was popular!

EPITAPHS

FOR several years I have been collecting old Sussex epitaphs and gravestone inscriptions. Some of these are genuine, and others probably not so, but they all give an insight, often quite light-hearted, into the attitude of Sussex folk towards their own and other people's demise. Here are just a few – some like the first very serious, but others surprisingly humorous.

This is how a group of young men were remembered in the nineteenth century in Kirdford churchyard:

> *To the memory of George Newman aged 17.*
> *Charles Newman aged 13.*
> *Thomas Rapley aged 14.*
> *George Puttick aged 13.*
> *and William Boxall aged 19 years.*
> *Who died at Sladeland on the 21st January 1838*
> *from having placed Green-wood ashes in their bedroom.*

Sometimes a moral was to be drawn when reading the epitaph, as in this one from Chichester:

> *Here lies a true soldier, whom all must applaud.*
> *Much hardship he suffered at home and abroad.*
> *But the hardest engagement he ever was in,*
> *was the battle of self in the conquest of sin.*

The following lines (or similar) have been credited to the poet William Hayley, but although he enjoyed writing epitaphs, his authority for this one is quite impossible. The words referring to a blacksmith have been noted in the churchyards at Felpham, Westbourne, Sidlesham, Stedham, Mid-Lavant and Hollington, and also in other counties:

> *My sledge and hammer lie reclined.*
> *My bellows too have lost their wind.*
> *My fire extinct; my forge decay'd,*
> *and in the dust my vice is laid.*
> *My coal is spent, my iron gone,*

The nails are druv - my work is done.

The humorous ones are perhaps the most suspect; for instance:

Here lies the body of Edward Hide,
We laid him here because he died.
We had rather,
It had been his father.
If it had been his sister,
We should have missed her.
But since 'tis honest Ned,
No more shall be said.

This was supposed to have been spotted in Storrington churchyard, but when it was looked for in 1861 it was not to be found.

The following was said to have graced a grave in a Downland churchyard:

Here lies the Mother of children seven.
Three on earth, and four in heaven.
The four in heaven preferring rather,
To be with Mother, than live with Father.

The next one has a full provenance, as it was written by a Mr Lee of the *Sussex Express*, for the grave of an illiterate horse-dealer of Lewes, a Mr Drowley:

Here lies a man that lived by lying.
Some people thought 'twould leave him dying.
But to the nation's great surprise,
Even in his grave he lies.

But can we really believe in this one?:

Here lies daughter Charlotte,
Who was born a virgin, and died a harlot.
For fifteen years she kept her virginity,
Not a bad record for this vicinity.

This sailor's tombstone, in Bosham churchyard, is in memory of Thomas Barrow, master of the sloop Two Brothers, who 'by the breaking of the horse, fell into the sea and waas drown'd' on October 13, 1759, at the age of twenty-five

Lastly another one which seems to have been a favourite, as somewhat similar versions have been noted in West Hampnett, Barnham, East Grinstead and Tillington churchyards:

> *Pain was my fortune, Physic my food.*
> *Groans my devotion, death did me good.*
> *When Christ my physician, considered it best.*
> *To ease me of pain, and give my soul rest.*

FAIRIES

IF WE can believe some accounts from the past, fairies were once common in our county, although I doubt whether many will claim to have seen them in recent times. It has been suggested that a belief in these little people could be a dim folk memory of an ancient race of tiny folk, long long vanished. But we need to go back only a century or so, to find Sussex people who believed that they existed. One man described them as 'little creatures rather bigger than a squirrel and not quite as large as a fox'. Another said they were 'liddle folk, not more than a foot high, and uncommon fond of dancing'. Evidence was provided by the fairy rings on the South Downs, although the nature writer Gilbert White said the cause was in the turf, as grass taken from the Downs to his garden brought the rings with it. The scientific explanation is that the rings are caused by a type of fungus, throwing seeds outwards, so that gradually an ever-increasing circle of brighter grass is formed.

But the old Sussex country folk knew differently. They believed that the rings were caused by the little people dancing, and that they often appeared overnight. Author Arthur Beckett knew rings which had occupied the same spot for several years – some measuring up to several hundreds of feet, although most were much smaller.

The dialect word for fairies is pharisces or farisees (the spelling is uncertain). Proof of their existence was claimed because they were mentioned in the Bible! Many names may be cited as examples of places frequented by the fairies; for instance Faygate, Pucks Church Parlour, Pookbourne, Pook Hole, Pook Ryde and Pook Hale. Harrow Hill at Patching was believed to be the last home of the little folk in Sussex, although other places also share this distinction.

Several superstitions are connected with the fairies. When churning butter, the farm wife would chant:

Come butter come,
Come butter come.
Peter stands at the gate,
Waiting for a butter cake,
Come butter come.

This was to persuade the perverse little people who were holding back the butter, to relent and allow it to form.

Even today the fairy's colour, which was green, has a certain amount of ill luck associated with it when worn by mere mortals. A rhyme went:

> *Those dressed in blue have lovers true,*
> *Those dressed in green and white are forsaken quite.*

The place in Sussex most often associated with the fairies is Chanctonbury Ring, although it is only on Midsummer Eve, that magical of all nights, when they can be seen.

The housewife's helper was Dobbs, or Master Dobbs, a good fairy who could often be persuaded to help the harassed dame with her many chores. But like all fairies he was quick-tempered so you had to be careful not to upset him.

Many stories tell of the Sussex fairies, although it has to be admitted that most of them have a familiar ring to those versed in general fairy lore. One of the best known Sussex stories is of a ploughman who one day heard a little voice calling out from a crack in the ground, 'Help, help'. When he enquired what was the trouble, the voice replied, 'I have been baking and have broken my peel'. The kindly ploughman suggested it should be handed up to him, and with the help of a few tin tacks it was repaired and returned to its fairy owner. He was rewarded by a bowl of sweet smelling liquid, which he found very appetising. When he told his mates about this, he was laughed to scorn, but the unbelievers became ill and died soon after. Fairies have always hated to be laughed at.

Fairies have a great interest in horses. A carter once noticed how fat his horses were becoming, so one night he hid in the stable to find out why. Soon he saw the fairies appear, each with a little bag of corn with which they fed the horses. Suddenly one said to another, 'I twet. Do you twet?' whereupon the annoyed carter jumped out of his hiding place and shouted, 'I'll make you twet, afore I've done with you'. But before he could reach them, they had disappeared. However the fairies didn't forget and from that day the carter's horses grew thin, until they were useless for work. Sometimes horses found in a sweaty state in the morning caused blame to be heaped on the fairies or witches. But this blame could have been more correctly directed towards the smugglers, who often borrowed horses for their nocturnal activities.

Another story very similar to the one about the carter's horses, has the fairies threshing corn for the farmer. When one of the 'helpful' little folk complains that he 'twets', the onlooked jumps out of his hiding place and shouts at them whereupon he is struck on the head, and only just manages to stagger home feeling very weak. In spite of the ministrations of the doctor, he becomes progressively worse and dies exactly a year later. Another similar tale concerning the rather dangerous help offered by fairies, is of the Sussex man who found every morning that wheat had been carried in to his barn. Stupidly not being content to let well alone, he hid and observed the little folk each carrying an ear of corn on his head. Once more one of them exclaimed, 'I do twet'. The farmer unwisely called out, 'If you sweat for an ear, what would you do for a sheaf?' The touchy fairies disappeared and never offered their help again.

A nicer story comes from Beeding, where two thieves once stole a pig, which they popped into a sack to carry it away. When they stopped for a break at the foot of Beeding Hill, they unwittingly put the sack down with its mouth over a hole in which lived a fairy. The little man released the pig and took its place in the sack. As the thieves climbed the hill, they were surprised to hear a voice saying, 'Dick, Dick, where are you?' Whereupon a second small voice replied, 'In a sack, pick-a-back, riding up Beeding Hill'.

It was once related that a fairy funeral had been witnessed at Park Mound, Pulborough, although this was not the only one, as William Blake told a friend that he had watched a similar event during his stay at Felpham. The little creatures were 'the size and colour of green and grey grasshoppers, bearing a body laid out on a rose-leaf'. He said they buried their fellow with suitable songs, and then disappeared. But we have to remember that Blake was a poet!

FIG GARDENS

ONCE a village near Worthing, Tarring is now part of the urban sprawl of greater Worthing. In spite of this it still manages to retain a large part of its own identity, and a surprising amount of folklore The best known legends concern the fig gardens, which in the nineteenth century were a popular tourist attraction. It was a favourite spot to take afternoon tea ('cream teas and all the figs you could eat'), and picture postcards were on sale to spread its fame. One of the trees was said to have been planted by Thomas-a-Becket, and a notice read: 'This fig tree is the oldest in England. It was planted 800 years ago.' Another notice claimed that a certain tree had been planted by Becket in 1162. There was also a popular story claiming that it was actually St Richard who had been responsible for the first fig trees. In fact the trees were mainly planted in 1745, although some may have been there before that date. The Fig Gardens were still open to the public in 1936, but closed after the Second World War. They were then sold, and later a residential development, Bishops Close, was built on the site. What remain of

The famous fig garden at Tarring in 1904

Avenues of fig trees at the Tarring garden

the fig trees are now in two private gardens, which are opened to the public on one day annually. One of the owners makes delicious fig jam, and provides her visitors with scones covered with this delicacy.

A further rather strange item of traditional lore is connected with the fig trees. It tells of an Italian bird called a beccafico, which descends on the trees when the fruit is ripe, and remains for just a week. Apart from a garden at Sompting, which also claims the visitor, nowhere else in England ever sees this bird (although I have to admit that I have not found anyone who can actually claim to have spotted the bird, even at Tarring). Experts say that the bird may really be a much more common species.

FIRING THE ANVIL

MENTIONED elsewhere in this book, the popular practice of firing the anvil has been well documented as a custom carried out by Sussex blacksmiths to mark all kinds of local, and national, occasions. These could range over relatively minor things such as local weddings to big national events such as jubilees and coronations.

In 1979 I asked Tom Holt to explain to me exactly how it was done. The anvil was upended and a hole in the bottom was plugged with gunpowder. A wooden peg was pushed in and carefully driven home. Then a gimlet was used to bore a hole through the peg, with the tool being plunged into cold water every few seconds (this was the most dangerous part). The hole then had a fuse inserted, which was lit when required. Those close by heard little of the explosion, but others at a distance had the benefit of a very loud report. Many tales tell of smiths who lost their eyebrows, hair or whiskers (and perhaps all three), although these minor setbacks seem to have had little effect on the popularity of the custom.

Many accounts from the past tell us how often the firing was carried out. In the diary of George Greenfield, estate carpenter at Balcombe Place (1875-84), we find a note that 'James Webber married, and his men were firing the anvil in the street'. In Petworth in the early 1900s, Mr Baxter the smith fired his anvil to celebrate the return of the Conservative candidate at the election. The result was described as 'like a coastguard's maroon'.

My old friend Scan Tester of Horsted Keynes remembered the custom being carried out at the Relief of Ladysmith, as must have happened in a great many Sussex villages. Scan said: 'She was a tidy rattle. We boys run for our lives'.

In 1953 Helena Hall of Lindfield, who loved old customs, noted that John Sharman, the Lindfield smith, fired his anvil for the coronation. He had previously marked the Relief of Mafeking and several jubilees and coronations in similar fashion.

F Holland, the Broadbridge Heath blacksmith, recalled in 1964 how his father had fired the anvil on the twenty-first birthday of a local gentleman's son. After several attempts, he gave the plug a final blow, and it went off suddenly, just missing his face. He was stripped of his shirt, and had gunpowder blown into his arms and hair. The

Frank Dean, the Rodmell blacksmith, fires the anvil to commemorate the Queen's Silver Jubilee in 1977

doctor got most of the specks out, except for one in the corner of his eye, which remained there until he died in 1908.

In quite modern times anvils have been fired when old customs were being revived. This was done at the behest of the Chanctonbury Morris Men at Pyecombe in 1962, when the chemist was asked to provide the powder, and was worried that he may have made it too strong. A report notes that 'much cyder was drunk'.

The date of the last event was November 23, Old Clem's Night, and the feast of St Clement, patron saint of Sussex blacksmiths, when an actor played the part of Old Clem.

When I wrote about Firing the Anvil in a Sussex newspaper quite recently my piece caught the eye of an American, who was a member of an anvil firing association. Apparently the custom has a number of adherents in the United States, although they carry it out in a rather different fashion. This American subsequently called on me during a visit to this country, and told me of his great enthusiasm for the custom.

GOOD FRIDAY

GOOD Friday was an important day in Sussex with many survivals of ancient customs and recreational activities, some of which continue into the present time. An alternative name was Marble Day, and romantics have suggested that the popularity of the playing marbles on this particular day could be a survival of the casting of lots for Christ's garments by means of knuckle bones by the Roman soldiers.

In recent times the marble championships at Tinsley Green and Battle have attracted attention, but 100 years ago marbles were played on Good Friday all over the county, from Bodiam, Northiam, Salehurst and Robertsbridge in the east, through Selmeston, Lewes, Cuckfield, Slaugham and Horsham, to West Chiltington, Sidlesham and Rogate in the west. The marble season really started on Ash Wednesday and continued until noon on Good Friday; after this time marbles were supposed to be put away until the following year, and anyone playing out of season could have their marbles snatched away with the cry of 'smugs' or a similar magical word.

Bat and Trap at The Level, Brighton, late 1930s

Henry Burstow of Horsham played marbles in the main street with other boys in the 1830s. In many villages of Sussex, large rings were scribed outside the main shops, with marbles heaped in the centre and left for any passerby to knock out.

At Slaugham a big ring was made outside some stable doors, and men, women and children played.

Sam Spooner, who was born in 1861, was one of the first players at Tinsley Green when the games were organised into the championship that we know today. According to Sam, marbles were first played here in the reign of Elizabeth I, when local lads played for the hand of a rosy-cheeked maid. More realistically we know that one of the most successful teams at Tinsley Green in the first years of the 'revival' was that of the Crawley Busmen, and they were largely responsible for the modern game that is still played there today. Sam McCarthy-Fox has made a study of marbles at Tinsley Green and elsewhere in Sussex, and he has written largely on the subject with knowledge that is unsurpassed.

The Marbles Championship at Battle, 1949

Not everyone was in favour of marble-playing. A Sussex vicar, writing in 1879, observed that his parishioners, playing marbles on Good Friday, continued their games at the very gate of the church until the last moment before the service began. As soon as it was over, they hurried out to continue for the rest of the time available.

Skipping was another game which became attached to Good Friday, and as the men played marbles, so in many towns and villages the women and children

104

skipped. Another name for the day (when it was not called Marbles Day) was Long Rope Day, or Long Line Day. The custom was particularly popular during the nineteenth century along the coast, and a few inland places close by. At Brighton, where the old fishing families kept up their time-honoured customs, it was particularly popular until the start of the Second World War. It took place on the fishmarket hard, and in nearby streets. The ropes used in Brighton probably came from the fishing boats, although at other places scaffold ropes, well ropes, clothes lines, and even hop vines were used. Skipping came to an end at Brighton when the fishmarket was closed by barbed wire in 1940, a minor casualty of the early days of the war.

Other places where skipping was popular included Hastings, Hove, Southwick and Lewes. Not far from Brighton, Patcham had a tradition of Good Friday skipping, where the farm labourers took turns to turn the rope while the rest of the village skipped, several at a time, throughout the day.

A lady from Ashurst Wood told me about the skipping in the village, with very thick ropes which were normally used by men in their work. During the morning the women organised the skipping, and then at midday the children skipped while the women held the rope. Mrs Loomes of Burgess Hill also gave me her recollections of Good Friday, when she even saw a one-legged man with crutches skipping.

Alciston was another popular place for communal skipping and Cyril Phillips of Cuckfield told me that after skipping around midday in the road outside the inn, the skipping folk walked to Berwick Woods to pick bluebells and primroses, before returning home by train to Lewes. Good Friday skipping still takes place outside the pub, Rose Cottage, at Alciston, arranged today by the Knots of May women's morris dancers who revived the custom in the mid 1970s.

Another Good Friday game was bat and trap (or to give it two of its other names – trap bat, or bat and ball). It was played in Brighton for longer than anyone can remember, although why it became associated with Good Friday nobody knows, as elsewhere it is played at indiscriminate times of the year, The rules are as follows: 'The ball is placed on the lever of the shoe-shaped trap, and is made to rise by a tap with the bat on the end of the lever, The batsman then attempts to strike it downwards in the direction of the fieldsmen who stand in a line. He is out if he fails to hit the ball after three attempts' I have heard the game described as a sort of cricket match without a wicket. It was played on the Level at Brighton just north of St Peter's Church, usually by teams from local public houses, and the Brighton Labour Club. The barrel of beer for the players was paid for by the losing team or by collections.

The rather unlikely game of kiss-in-the-ring was yet another popular Good Friday sport. It was played near Brighton, and at Hastings, Seaford and Southwick; at the latter place it was accompanied by the sale of gilt gingerbread. Kiss-in-the-ring was also played in Sussex at other times of the year. One man told man how the Worthing flower show always ended with the main tent being cleared so that the younger folk could indulge in a positive frenzy of the game, and that many met their future spouses on that occasion.

Buns baked for Good Friday were sometimes kept until the following year in tin boxes, as this was considered a way to retain good luck. Sometimes the buns, which were said to keep their goodness, were hung up in cottages, and a piece would then be broken off as required and pounded up as a medicine. Keeping one

Skipping at Brighton, Good Friday, 1936

in the house was also regarded as a precaution against fire. The well known rhyme went:

> Hot Cross Buns, Hot Cross Buns,
> One a penny, Two a penny,
> Hot cross Buns, all hot, all hot, all hot.
> If you haven't any daughters, give them to your sons.
> If you haven't of these merry little elves,
> Then you may need them for yourselves.

Bread baked on Good Friday was also said to remain without mould, and miniature loaves were sometimes baked for children to keep. Good Friday buns and bread were taken to sea by fishermen as a safeguard against disaster. In recent times, I was told of a man who bought a secondhand car, and found an un-mouldy hot cross bun secreted in the glove compartment.

Good Friday Hill at Shoreham is said to have been given this name because of an old custom of rolling hard-boiled eggs down the slope behind the church on Good Friday. Before being rolled the eggs were painted in bright colours. The tradition of painting eggs at Easter, although found in Sussex, does seem to have been much stronger in the northern counties. The symbolic association of the egg with the resurrection is well known. It has also been suggested that the rolling egg may represent the rolling away of the stone from Christ's tomb.

For those who prefer work to play on Good Friday, it will probably not be necessary to remind them that this is the traditional day for planting seed potatoes.

GOODING

GOODING or Going-a-Gooding was a gentle custom once observed each year on St Thomas's Day (December 21). This must have been the start of Christmas for many less well-off older people, for they were encouraged to call on their better-off neighbours to collect gifts to make the festive season just a little bit more enjoyable. Those who were well endowed with life's luxuries fully expected to be asked for a contribution of food or money, and apparently few of them said no.

There were some nice stories which reveal how the custom was carried out. Henry Burstow of Horsham tells us, in his *Reminiscences*, that Sir Timothy Shelley of Field Place used to give beef away in large quantities; R Aldridge of St Leonard's Forest gave about six pounds of beef and a plum pudding to sixty or seventy families; and Mrs Fox of Chestnut Lodge gave a quarter of a pound of tea, and two and sixpence in cash to about eighty poor old women, and two ounces of tea and a shilling in cash to about 200 more. The vicar of Upper Beeding used to sit at his study window on December 21, with a pile of silver in front of him. The old women would curtsey in thanks as they received their share. Presumably they were also expected to turn up at church on the following Sunday. Lady Hurst wrote of the custom in 1889, commenting on the old people wearing scarlet cloaks and black satin bonnets to receive their dole – surely someone was responsible for this special mode of dress for the occasion. Sometimes the old folk, when receiving their gifts, offered a sprig of holly in exchange, so it seems that much of the giving was well organised.

Later the shops took up the custom, previously the responsibility of the gentry. A Horsham shopkeeper in the 1930s filled the back portion of his ironmongers shop (opening on to the Carfax) with logs each December, so that the poor and old could take what they required. A writer in 1922 said that the custom 'now seems entirely dropped', so apart from shopkeepers, it would appear to have ceased by about the beginning of the twentieth century. Surprisingly, a Sussex woman told me just a few years ago that in Lewes, one could still hear the term gooders applied to those who gave gifts at Christmas.

GROTTOS AND GROTTO DAY

JULY 25 is the Feast Day of St James and was once known as Grotto Day, when pilgrims who could not visit his shrine at Compostella in Spain made shell grottos in his honour. His emblem was a scallop shell, and these were worn by pilgrims. By the last century it seems to have become purely a children's custom, when they made shell grottos in the streets, with the intention of exacting pennies from generous adults. Their rhyme was:

> *Please to remember the grotto,*
> *It's only once a year.*
> *Fathers gone to sea,*
> *Mothers gone to fetch him back,*
> *So please remember me.*

At Brighton the day seems to have become confused with August 5 when oysters come into season, and grottos using oyster shells appeared in the streets of the town. In 1883 a writer reported seeing them within the preceding twenty years, although by the twentieth century the custom appears to have disappeared in Sussex. Strangely it has been reported from London in more modern times.

Another treasured item of folklore connected with July 25 is that on that day chicory may be used to render its wearer invisible.

A much more grand shell grotto was built by Sarah, the second Duchess of Richmond, and her two daughters at Goodwood House, in the 1730s. They used shells from the West Indies and other exotic parts of the world, with the walls being covered with coloured shells, the floor being paved with black and white marble, and with panels of horses teeth. A mirror in an alcove was designed to reflect the spire of Chichester Cathedral. The work took seven years to complete, and was opened to the public in the early around 100 years ago. Many shells were taken by visitors, and had to be replaced.

HARVEST HOME

WHEN the final load of the harvest was brought in, the men would chant:

> *We've ploughed, we've sowed,*
> *We've ripped, we've mowed.*
> *We've carried our last harvest load,*
> *And never overthrowed. Hip, Hip, Hooray.*

If the harvest had been a good one, then the 'hollerin' pot' would be called for. This was an extra ration of ale for all the workers, although this would be missing if the last load had 'over throwed' or gone wrong in some way.

At Rottingdean the last sheaf was carried round the village, with the men calling at all the pubs. This would have been loaded on to a decorated wagon drawn by four proud horses wearing their bells. Standing in the cart was the bailiff of Challoners Farm, old Brasser Copper, shouting out the time-honoured words.

On most of the larger farms a harvest supper was provided by the

A harvest time picture from North Bersted, c1908

110

farmer on a Saturday evening, so that the men had Sunday to get over their jollifications. The largest barn would be pressed into service for the feast, with the barn doors taken off their hinges and used as table tops. Sometimes the supper would be for the whole village, with all the big landowners contributing. Most were happy about this, although not all were so generous. One squire's Harvest Home consisted of two buns for the children, plus a drink of tea (but they had to provide their own mugs).

But mostly the suppers were organised on a much more generous scale. At Wiston the great coach house was used, and in an old book by Matthew Coombe, *Memories of Wiston*, a picture is painted of all who worked on the estate attending in their best Sunday smocks, each bringing their own knife and fork. The tables groaned under ribs of roast beef, and 'Wissen' home brewed' was carried round in a pail, and drunk from horn mugs. The evening ended with 'Wissen' plum pudding.

Doris Hall, in her book on Streat and Westmeston, speaks of an annual custom at the supper held in the great barn at Place Farm. At the end of the feast, the farmer's wife brought in a huge seed cake. The farmer would cut this, and tell his wife who should be given a slice. Those who were left out knew that their services would not be needed in the following year. This must have clouded an otherwise happy occasion for a few of those present.

But mainly these were happy evenings, with drink flowing freely, and songs and games following the feast.

Toasts were an essential part of any successful harvest supper. Typical ones were 'A barn full and rent paid', or 'More corn and less rats'. A shy boy called upon to propose a toast for the first time, could fall back on this bit of rustic wit, 'Scorched bread, well buttered. If that bain't toast, then I'm buggered. '

Many of the songs which were brought out regularly each year by the same singers, were also games with forfeits. For instance, while merrymakers were singing 'Of all the horses in the Merry Green Wood, 'twas the bob-tail mare carried the bells away', the words ho, re, wo and gee had to be sung in turn by different singers, and those who missed had to pay a forfeit. Another old favourite was *Turn the Cup Over*. In this the man next to the chairman received a cup of beer on the crown of his hat. He had to drink this without touching the cup, then throw the utensil into the air and catch it in his hat.

Felpham Harvest Home, 1869

Meanwhile the company sang the song which ended 'the liquor's drinked up, and the cup is turned over'. If the player failed to perform correctly, then the singers would change the last line to '. . . and the cup ain't turned over'. Then the cup was refilled and the player went through the whole thing again. Everyone took a turn, so the performance must have taken up a large part of the evening. One observer said he went home thoroughly bored with the repetition of this rigmarole.

A number of other songs were associated with the harvest feasts, such as *The Jolly Woodcutter*, which in its second verse sums up the feelings of all present – or so the farmer hoped:

> *Here's a health unto our Master, the founder of our feast.*
> *I wish him well with all my heart, that his soul in heaven*
>   *may rest.*
> *That all his work may prosper, whatever he takes in hand.*
> *For we are all his servants, and all at his command.*

And so we leave the honest farm workers of the past, with the words of an old poem recited at Wiston:

> *And later on in the cool evening twilight,*
> *They'd wend their way home with a hearty good-night.*

HERMITS AND ANCHORITES

THE remains of men and women apparently walled up in old buildings may not have been of criminals, but anchorites who preferred a solitary life rather than the cares of the world. There were several Sussex men and women who opted for this kind of religious contemplation.

There were said to be anchorites at Pagham, Houghton, Stopham, Hardham, Findon and, possibly the earliest one, at Lewes. He was Magnus, said to have been of royal Danish descent. One legend says that King Harold ended his life as a recluse close to a church in Chester, although this is most likely a piece of historical confusion.

Many of the anchorites had their cells adjacent to churches, with a squint in the inside wall so that they could see the celebration of Mass. Some of these cells have disappeared, but the squint remains in the church wall. There was often a special service of dedication, with the bishop placing his seal upon the cell door. These holy men and women depended on locals to provide them with the bare essentials of food and drink, and spent their whole life in prayer and meditation.

The Reverend William Bolle, Rector of St Leonard's at Aldrington, near Hove, suddenly announced in 1402 that he was to become an anchorite or hermit until the end of his life. A roomy cell was constructed in the churchyard, adjoining his church. There he remained for a number of years, occasionally glimpsed by his parishioners, and with a growing reputation for holiness. There was a doubtful story that his cell was subsequently moved to a spot adjoining Chichester Cathedral, where alms would have been more plentiful.

Steyning is reputed to have had a female anchorite, Miliana, who had a reputation for bad temper. She sued Richard of Hardham, another anchorite, for money which she said he owed to her. Later she sued the Prior of Hardham for food which she said should have been provided. Afterwards she is reputed to have gone to law on several occasions in support of her 'rights'.

That the life of a hermit was not an unhealthy one is shown by the age of many of them. Some stayed in their cells for forty or fifty years, and one is reputed to have remained in seclusion for ninety-seven years.

Brightling Needle

Of a rather different kind were the hermits, engaged to live in caves or other follies built by landowners, to enhance their estates. Most of these probably gave up such an artificial life after a short time. When a hermit was advertised for to inhabit Brightling Needle, one of Squire John Fuller's follies, the conditions stated that he had to stay for at least a year, and not to shave, cut his hair or wash. He also had to refrain from contact with anyone; not difficult one would think, in view of his personal habits. But there were no takers.

HILL FIGURES

UNDOUBTEDLY the best known hill figure in Sussex is that of the Long Man of Wilmington, on Windover Hill, three miles west Eastbourne and south of the A27. Much has been written about the old man's age and origin, and experts disagree on both. Dates suggested range from pre-historic times to post-medieval. To make things more difficult, the figure has been renovated many times. The giant is said to be the largest human figure of this kind in the country.

Romantic legends link the figure to the Holy Grail, and there are said to be dim memories of two figures, known as Adam and Eve. The best known folk stories certainly tell of two giants, one on Windover Hill and one on Firle Beacon. They are said to have hurled rocks at each other, with the Windover giant being killed and buried where the outline remains.

Cyril Phillips, who once farmed at Firle, told me that when he first came to Sussex as a ten-year-old in the 1920s, he met a one- armed shepherd who tended his flock on the Downs near Alfriston. His story was just a little different from the above. As he told it, there were two giants, one on Windover and one on Mount Caburn. They were both flint-workers, and they used to chat to each other across the valley. On day they fell out and the Caburn Giant threw his flint hammer and knocked out the Long Man, and they buried him where he died.

Cyril wrote a monologue about the events, which included these lines:

> There was an argument, one day he said.
> And the Wilmington man yelled 'You ought to be dead'.
> Now this riled the giant on Mount Caburn Hill,
> And for quite a while he stood perfectly still.
> Then up with his hammer and took a good aim,
> To hit his opponent and just make him lame.

Another legend is that the figure is of a giant killed by pilgrims on their way to Wilmington Priory. Yet a third story is that the giant is a memorial of a visit paid to Sussex by St Peter. As if to add weight to this very unlikely tale, as late as 1870 local people claimed to be able

The Long Man of Wilmington

to make out a cock to the right of the figure (this being the emblem of St Peter).

The two staffs held by the Long Man may once have been quite different. A 1766 sketch shows the two implements as a rake and a scythe. Another suggestion is that they could have been crosses, which were added to a pre-Christian figure.

We have still not exhausted the suggestions as to the figure's origin. Some say it was the site of an ancient sacrificial site, a tribute to an ancient chief, a medieval direction sign to Wilmington Priory– or even part of a huge sundial. It seems that anyone looking for a definitive origin has an almost impossible task.

A local weather rhyme goes like this:

> *When Firle or Long Man wear a cap,*
> *We in the valley gets a drap.*

The 'drap' is, of course, rain, which follows a cloud seen over the hills.

Other Sussex hill figures include the White Horse on Hindover Hill between Alfriston and Seaford. The original horse of 1838 was

116

reputed to have been cut in a single day to mark the Coronation of Queen Victoria, by a party of young men on a picnic, or alternatively by James Pagden of Alfriston, and his brothers. This is confirmed in a book written by Pagden's daughter. The horse was still visible in the late 1800s. Some reject the Coronation theory and say it was intended as a memorial to a girl who was killed when her horse bolted down the hill, throwing her to her death.

A second white horse was cut in 1924 by JT Ade with help from his friends on one moonlit night. This is 100 yards south east of the first, and some believe it was merely intended to be a tidying of the first horse. Below it there was added a large letter S. The horse was covered during the war, and restored in 1945-9.

The white horse appears frequently in Sussex folklore, often as a symbol of luck.

A green cross cut in the turf on the Downs near Plumpton is mentioned by many older writers on Sussex. The official story of this was that it was to mark the site of the Battle of Lewes in 1264, although some locals prefer the more romantic story that the cross was a guide for the Crusaders on their way to the Holy Land. There is also a belief that the cross was once cut in chalk.

Better known is the large V of trees, further along the same range, above Streat, which was planted in 1887 to mark Queen Victoria's Golden Jubilee. Originally a letter R was to have been included, but the cost could not be raised. The V covers one and a half acres, each arm is 165 yards long and twenty-two yards wide. It was planted with 1,200 Scots pines, 800 spruce, 400 larch, 400 beech, 299 sycamore, twenty limes and forty Austrian pines. During World War Two it was suggested that the trees be felled as they might serve as a marker for German bombers.

HOWLING THE FRUIT TREES

AROUND Christmas or the New Year (especially on the Eve of the Epiphany) gangs of men and boys would visit the Sussex orchards, to wassail the fruit trees, wishing them good health for the coming season. Wassail means 'be whole'. The wassailing, or 'worsling' was often referred to in Sussex as howling, possibly because of the sounds made by the howlers with their cow horns, various kitchen utensils, and even guns loaded with powder. This was all to scare away any evil spirits that might be lurking in the branches of the trees. Several rhymes were recited, such as:

> *Stand fast root, bear well top.*
> *Pray the Gods send us a good howling crop.*
> *Every twig, apples big.*
> *Every bough, apples enow.*
> *Hats full, caps full, my pockets full too.*
> *Full quarter sacks full.*
> *Holla boys, holla. Huzzah.*

Another version (and there were several) was:

> *Here stands a good old apple tree,*
> *Stand fast root, bear well top.*
> *Every twig, apples big.*
> *Every bough, apples now.*
> *Hats full, caps full,*
> *Four and twenty sacks full.*
> *Hip Hip Hooray.*

Just to seal the bargain, toasts were drunk in Sussex cider punch, and the guns would be fired into the branches.

The Reverend Giles Moore of Horsted Keynes, writing in his diary in the seventeenth century, noted: 'I gave the Howling Boys Sixpence'. And another diarist, Timothy Burrell of Cuckfield, wrote, in 1691: 'A shilling paid to Howlers on New Years Eve'. Herrick wrote in his poem *Hesperides:*

Wassail the trees, that they may beare
you, many a plum and many a pear.
For more of less fruits they will bring,
as you do give them Wassailing.

The custom gradually faded, and was mostly obsolete in Sussex by the end of the nineteenth century. Mrs Powell of Portslade recalled that by this time the wassailing ritual was carried out by children only. One place in Sussex where wassailing continued later than elsewhere was at Duncton, near Chichester. Thanks to the efforts of Richard 'Spratty' Knight, the local miller, it continued each Twelfth Night into the twentieth century. In 1919 the *West Sussex Gazette* noted that although Spratty's son, Arthur, had done his best to keep things alive, the wassailing that year was attended by only three others. An interesting picture survives showing Richard Knight, standing under an apple tree, evidently ready for the 'howling' to take place. He is dressed in an elaborate suit with a bright flowery pattern, and with a string of apples round his neck, and a large decorated hat also bearing apples. His wife is beside him holding a cake on a plate, and a jug presumably containing cider. Arthur is also present, wearing a hat decorated with apples.

Richard Knight's great-grandson, Richard Holmwood, told me of an anecdote handing down in the family, that every day after work Richard would drive his horse and cart to the Cricketers Arms and stay there until closing time. One day he died while out on his rounds, and the horse carried him not to his home, but to the usual place, the pub. This was January 1908, just three days before the next wassailing.

The original custom may have died out in the county, but it has been revived in several places in modern times by Sussex Morris Men, notably at Henfield and Sompting.

JACOB'S POST

THE eighteenth century in Sussex was noted for a number of barbaric crimes, equalled only by the barbaric punishments meted out to the perpetrators. A public hanging was not considered entertaining enough, but was followed by the encasing of the murderer's body in a metal cage, which was then suspended near the scene of the crime, to become a reminder to others who might consider the same path to crime.

This is the story of Jacob Harris, a Jewish pedlar who in following his trade stayed at several Sussex inns. In May 1734 he lodged at the Royal Oak, Ditchling Common, where the landlord was Richard Miles. Rumours were rife that Miles had a secret cache of gold secreted somewhere in the inn, and this was too much for the avaricious soul of Jacob. While the unfortunate landlord was attending to the horses in the stables, Jacob pounced on him and

Jacob's Post on Ditchling Common

tried to cut his throat with a twopenny knife. Leaving his victim apparently dead, he went back into the inn but was accosted by a servant girl, whom he despatched in a similar fashion. Searching for the innkeeper's treasure, he came upon Richard's wife ill in bed. Evidently thinking that three murders were no worse than two, he killed her with the same knife.

Meanwhile the innkeeper, although in a bad way, was not quite dead. With difficulty he raised the alarm, and the murderer, fearing for his liberty, made his escape, riding as far as Turners Hill. Here he was discovered at an inn, overpowered and taken into custody.

At Horsham in August 1734 Jacob Harris was condemned to death for 'murders most foul'. After his execution he was put into the gibbet cage and exhibited on Ditchling Common near to the scene of his crimes. Part of the gibbet remained until at least 1882. When the original collapsed, the remains were taken to the inn and carefully preserved. Pieces of this grisly relic soon acquired a reputation as a charm against evil spirits, and accidents and diseases of all sorts, particularly toothache and fits. One old woman swore by the properties of the charm, and carried a piece of the wood with her for the rest of her life. William Albery, the Horsham historian, quoted an old native of Ditchling who said: 'People come from moiles and moiles and moiles to get a bit of that poisty, so as they shouldn't faul in these yere fits.'

Local entrepreneurs had contributed to the collapse of the original gibbet post by cutting pieces from it to sell to the gullible. When the original had completely disappeared, a facsimile was erected, the first of several. The replica was topped by a cockerel made of iron, with the date 1734 cut into it. Wooden rails around the post did not remain long, being removed by local gypsies for firewood.

This was when public executions always had their attendant attractions, such as a hang fair, and the sale of broadside ballads purporting to be the true account of the crime – and often the murderer's confession. The ballad relating Jacob's execution, included the following:

> At Horsham Gallows he was hanged there,
> On 31st August that same year.
> And where he did the crime, they took the pains,
> To bring him back and hang him up in chains.

Needless to say Jacob's Post attracted all kinds of supernatural tales. Ethel Powell told me a story which she had from her grandfather. One night the village lads were joking about the ghost of Jacob, and one of the bolder was persuaded to spend some time at the post that very night. What he didn't know was that some of the others where hiding in wait for him, and when he bravely asked, 'Hello Jacob, how are you tonight?' a gruff voice replied, 'Very wet

121

and cold'. The victim took to his heels and was not seen again for some time. This is an example of how tales of this kind circulate, and become attached to more than one locality, as very similar stories have been told to me about another gibbet post at Burpham.

Ursula Ridley, in *The Story of a Forest Village - West Hoathly*, (1971) tells a tale concerning Selsfield House, where Jacob Harris was said to have taken refuge when he was on the run. This house gained the reputation of being haunted as a result of having harboured a murderer.

A facsimile of Jacob's Post may still be seen today, although as far as I know there are no modern accounts of ghostly happenings.

This is a replacement of the original 1734 post on Ditchling Common

JUG AND MUG RHYMES

WE DO not know who was the first person to think of putting a rhyme or some other piece of homespun philosophy on a household jug or mug, but we owe him (or her) a debt for the pleasure these objects have given us, with their glimpses of the past. Here are just a few of these nostalgic reminders of Sussex yesterdays.

An early example in Brighton Museum, an earthenware beaker, offers this warning:

> From rocks and sands and barren lands,
> Good Father set me free.
> And for great guns and women's tongues,
> Good Lord deliver me.

Not everyone will be quite so rash as to equate women's tongues with Great Guns, and what can we make of this, from a mug dated 1735, found in a chimney of an old Horsham house:

> Hard very hard; the life of a man is but a span,
> But a woman's life a yard.

The finder of this was rewarded, as when found the mug contained a sum of money.

Very comforting is the inscription on a jar in the Sussex Archaeological Society's Barbican Museum in Lewes:

> My tobacco I do put,
> Within this little pot.
> And my friends can have a pipe.
> If any I have got.

Well you cannot say fairer than that. My mother recalled a mug also in same museum, which carried this bit of homely wisdom:

> Of a little, take a little,
> You are welcome there unto.
> But of a little, leave a little.
> For tis manners, so to do.

Worthing Museum has two mugs owned by miller Oliver of Highdown Mill, who was reputed to be a smuggler. He liked making up his own rhymes, and these are probably both originally penned by him.

> Money makes the mare to go,
> And so it does the mill.
> An honest man will pay when he can,
> But a rogue he never will.

> On Highdown Hill there stands a mill,
> The miller is honest you will find.
> For he takes toll from both great and small,
> Who send their corn to grind.

One of the commonest inscriptions on mugs (even at the present day) is the well known Farmer's Creed. This, of course, is also found in other counties.

> Let the wealthy and great,
> Roll in splendour and state.
> I envy them not, I declare it.
> I eat my own lamb,
> My own chicken and ham,
> I shear my own fleece and I wear it.
> I have lawns, I have bowers,
> I have fruits, I have flowers,
> The lark is my morning alarmer.
> So jolly boys now,
> Here's God speed the plough,
> Long life and success to the farmer.

The creed tends to differ slightly wherever it is found, and is also popular as a toast. I first heard it recited by Tinker Smith, who plied his trade on the Sussex-Surrey border, in the 1950s.

Many mugs were produced for the Diamond Jubilee of Queen Victoria, but there was one which had a particular Sussex connection as it showed the Queen on one side, and the Mayor of Lewes on the other.

LOGS AND WOOD

WOOD features widely in Sussex folklore, not surprisingly when we consider the important place that this material played in our ancestor's daily lives. Oak has been called the Sussex weed, so perhaps this is a good reason to give it pride of place.

In one version of the very popular poem *Logs to Burn*, which many Sussex folk will know, the list of woods begins with 'Oak logs will warm you well, If they're old and dry'. But oak is not always popular, as a rhyme about storms warns us, 'Beware of the oak, It draws the stroke'.

Maple was supposed to have the virtue of bestowing long life on children who were passed through its branches. When rumour had it that a maple tree in West Grinstead Park was to be cut down, a petition was drawn up for it to be spared.

Ash is sometimes less popular. In the storm rhyme, it was said 'Avoid the ash, it courts the flash (but creep under the thorn, it can save you from harm). However the ash was also said to have supernatural healing powers, and Spencer spoke of it as being 'for nothing ill'.

Charlotte Latham of Fittleworth, in her *West Sussex Superstitions*

Queen Elizabeth's Oak at Northiam

Lingering in 1868, says that the most singular superstition connected with the ash, is the belief that burying a shrew alive, in a hole bored in the tree, would remedy certain ills supposedly inflicted by the little rodent on man or beast. Once people in West Sussex spoke of the 'pink-nosed mouse' as a thing of evil omen. Not so far away from Sussex the Vicar of Selborne destroyed a 'shrew-mouse tree' that had stood long by the parsonage, believing that by rooting up the tree he would root out of the minds of his parishioners, their superstitious belief in its virtues.

But when we start thinking of the Christmas yule logs, then it is ash which is said to burn well even when green, as this couplet tells us:

> *Ash wood wet and ash wood dry,*
> *A king may warm his slippers by.*

A bundle of ash branches, bound together, was often used as kindling for the Christmas fire, when it was lit on Christmas Eve. Another saying was 'Burn ash wood green, fit for a Queen'.

Logs to Burn usually begins in this way:

> *Logs to burn, logs to burn.*
> *Logs to save the coal a turn,*
> *Here's a word to make you wise,*
> *When you hear the woodman's cries,*
> *Never heed his usual tale,*
> *That he has splendid logs for sale.*
> *But read these lines and generally learn.*
> *The proper kind of logs to burn.*

The unknown poet then goes on to detail all the logs that you may think of using such as oak, beech, yew, chestnut, hawthorn, elm, holly, apple, pear and cherry. But the lines usually end with praise for the ash, as in this version:

> *But ash logs all smooth and grey,*
> *Burn them green and old.*
> *Buy up all that come your way.*
> *They're worth their weight in gold.*

MAY DAY

FROM a pre-Christian spring time fertility festival, through to more modern centuries with the emphasis on children and May garlands, and back to a custom now celebrated widely by sturdy morris men, May 1 has always been a day quite different from other annual holidays. For obvious reasons spring time has always represented rebirth and natural fertility. With the Romans it was a feast day dedicated to Flora, the goddess of flowers.

In the Middle Ages Bringing in the May was the most widely practised custom, with men and women going to the woods to return with greenery and blossom.

In the seventeenth century Puritans banned such customs, and the most puritanical, Philip Stubbs, spoke of 'this stinking idol', meaning the old English tall maypole. Perhaps he had some justification, as a contemporary writer said that of 100 girls who went into the woods on May Day, but a third returned as virgins.

The maiden who on the first of May,
Goes to the fields at the break of day.
And washes in dew from the hawthorn tree,
Shall ever afterwards beautiful be.

But in spite of censure, May Day was still celebrated, especially by milkmaids and chimney sweeps.

Few of the traditional maypoles have survived, certainly none in Sussex. It was the Victorians with their love of Olde England who revived some of the customs, ignoring the Pagan side. In the nineteenth century May Day became popular as a children's festival, and with encouragement from adults, the May garlands (which had a respectable pedigree from at least the eighteenth century) became immensely popular.

Many accounts speak of how Garland Day was kept up in Sussex. Arthur Garner of Horsham told me in 1960, how May Day was celebrated in his childhood. The boys would go with a bunch of flowers, perhaps even weeds, to a big house in Clarence Road, where they would receive a halfpenny. The same boys would go several times, dressed a little differently each time (such as their caps back to front), and would always get their halfpenny.

Clara Chandler told me in 1980 that in Fletching the arrangements of flowers were always called maypoles, rather than garlands. The rhyme here went as follows:

The First of May is Maypole Day,
So please remember the Maypole.
We don't come here, but once a year,
So please remember the Maypole.

The children willingly walked a mile to Sheffield Park, for a competition on the lawn, with the winners being presented with a shilling.

At Slaugham there was a prize for the best garland, with a parade to the church for a special service. The children then paraded to the large houses for payment in money or food and drink. Mr Appleby of Tilgate Forest gave each child a penny, and because of this he was known as 'A penny for you, Appleby'. The chant here was 'Please, you want to see the maypole'. It was said that eventually the local school teacher killed the custom, calling the children 'beggars and cadgers'. Mrs M Lovely of Littlehampton told me in 1979 that she remembered the festival as May Doll Day. Girls would put a favourite doll in a box, decorated with silk or lace, plus suitable flowers. They then covered this with something like a lace curtain, and would knock on doors saying, 'Who would like to see the May doll?' If they were lucky, they received a penny, which might be saved for Christmas presents later in the year.

Another woman told me how a chair covered with flowers was prepared for a young May Queen with her garland, the 'throne' being lowered into the well to keep the flowers fresh for May Day. Rather a damp seat for the young May Queen I should think.

In 1889 a writer referred to the May garland custom as having died out, although it almost certainly went on well into the twentieth century. It seems impossible to say when the garland custom actually started, but it is recorded that several little girls carried garlands to an inn in Brighton in 1771. The Prince of Mecklenburg-Strelitz, who was staying there for his health, gave each of the children half a guinea.

Garland Day was revived in Lewes in 1980 by the Knots of May women's morris team, and continues to this day, with children's garlands being judged by the mayor in the castle's Gun Garden on Easter Monday.

Wearing a spray of lilies of the valley for your loved one on May Day, was a rather attractive custom noted by Dick Playll in Sussex. A much older custom which survived into Victorian days included the Jacks in the Green, popular with the chimney sweeps. In Horsham, Henry Burstow said that there were two sets of Jacks when he was a boy, the Potter and the Whiting parties. They paraded the town dressed in fancy costumes, accompanied by a fiddler. During the day they got merrier and merrier, until in the evening they retired the worse for wear to Whiting's beershop.

Burstow also left us an account of old Mrs Smallwood, who made her living selling milk. On May Day she would go around with an immense garland on a trolley drawn by boys. On top of the garland would be a little model cow. Dressed in bows and ribbons she would accompany her garland calling on all the principal residents. This old woman lived to be nearly 100, and until she was ninety-six regularly carried milk to her customers in buckets suspended from a yoke on her shoulders. The Jack in the Green Festival has a strong local connection in Hastings, and is now enjoying a splendid revival.

Children with their may garlands at Cowfold in 1912

Lewes Garland Day, 1982

At Brighton the fishermen went out on May Day with their boats decorated, and they considered it particularly lucky if it coincided with the mackerel season.

Nowadays we are used to seeing little girls (and sometimes older ones) crowned on May Morning as May Queen. This pleasant modern revival harks back to the old woodland festivals, when an attempt was made by the church to supplant the pagan queen with the Blessed Virgin.

Dancing round the maypole was once popular with adults, utilising the old tall maypoles decorated with greenery. The modern version is carried out by children, using smaller maypoles, from which are suspended brightly coloured ribbons. These are then plaited in a dance said to have been brought to this country in Victorian days from the continent. It has now become quintessentially English, with many folk recalling it from their school days in the 1920s. There have been many modern revivals of May festivities in Sussex, notably at Shoreham, Chichester, Lewes and Hastings, as well as other places.

Other folklore associated in Sussex with May, is that it is on the whole an unlucky month, with many witches abroad on May Day Eve. It was particularly unlucky to bring green broom into the house in May.

If you sweep the house with broom on May,
You'll sweep the head of the house away.

MILLS AND MILLERS

MUCH of the Sussex folklore connected with mills concerned the millers, but first of all here are a few items relating to the actual mills. The sails (sweeps) were often used to pass messages, and to indicate either good luck, celebration, mourning, or just that work was over for the day. If the miller were into smuggling, then the sails were very useful to signal to boats at sea. When two mills were on one site they were usually known as Jack and Jill, the best known pair being at Clayton. The two mills at Outwood Common, were also similarly known. Local wags would say that two mills on one hill would exhaust the available wind. When mills had to be moved (as they sometimes were), oxen were called in to provide the pulling power, as their great strength was capable of producing a more slow but steady movement than horses.

Not surprisingly many mills were supposed to be haunted. Clayton's mills had this reputation, and there were tales of bells ringing without reason in the miller's cottage. There was also supposed to be a 'secret tunnel' from the granary near by, to one of the mills. Jolesfield Mill at Partridge Green, was said to be haunted before it was later transported to Crawley.

The mill at Chalvington was apparently haunted by the ghost of a miller who had hanged himself on his own mill post. As was the custom, he was buried close by with a stake through his body. In 1829 the ghost was laid by some locals, who when digging found his bones.

Several mills had nicknames, for instance Hilaire Belloc called his mill 'Mrs Shipley'. The millwright who built this mill in 1879 was a large man named Grist, and I can recall my mother and aunts using the local phrase 'as fat as Old Grist'.

Several old guide books on Sussex have reported that the centre post of Salvington Mill is a living tree, although this is obviously untrue. However the saying that Chailey Mill is the centre of Sussex, is probably fairly close to the truth.

Parts of mills are usually spoken of as either 'he' or 'she' by millers, for example a millstone is feminine, whereas a ladder ,masculine. The actual names were often unique, such as the delightful word 'damsel' which is a small tray on a spring.

Now for a look at the millers, who were often eccentrics. William

Coombs of East Blatchington swore that a statement made by him was true, and if it were not then he would never enter his mill again. It proved to be false, and for the rest of his life he was said to have instructed his workforce from the mill steps. He was the character who painted his horse in different colours, depending on his mood.

A miller at Rodmell was reputed to hate church bells. One day he was disturbed by the local bells, and he cursed both the church and the smith who made the bells. Years later he lost his way in floods, and only found his way home by following the sounds of the Rodmell bells. Filled with contrition, he presented the church with a new set.

Jack, one of two
windmills at Clayton

Tom Hurst of Rectory Manor Mill, Eastbourne was locally reputed to be the strongest man in his area. When a quarrelsome gypsy offered to fight Tom, he invited the man to stand on the palm of his hand. When the traveller did so, Tom lifted his hand and crashed the man's head through the ceiling. At least that's the story.

Millers had a reputation for mean dealing, or even dishonesty. It was said that an honest miller had a tuft of hair in the palm of each hand. When challenged to show it, one miller replied that only honest men were capable of seeing it.

But for the most eccentric miller of them all, we must turn to John Oliver, miller of Highdown Hill, near Worthing. He designed his own tomb in 1776, and occupied it in 1793. Previously he had kept his coffin under his bed, so that it could be brought out immediately it was needed. On his coffin he was supposed to have written these lines:

> Beneath my bed my coffin stands,
> On four wheels swift it runs,
> I am always proud to show the same,
> And why my neighbours do you me blame.

His tomb may still be seen on the hill, although it has been vandalised by an earth-moving machine in modern times, and has had to be thoroughly renovated. Miller Oliver was reputed to be a smuggler, scripture student, poet and inventor. Regarding his smuggling activities, the story went that he used his capacious tomb to store some of the contraband. He had a passion for inscriptions, and there were many on his tomb. On another of his buildings he had the following:

> Stranger enjoy this sweet enchanting scene,
> The pleasing landscapes and the velvet green.
> Yet though the eye delighted rove,
> Think of the better scene above.

The Miller's Tomb at Highdown, near Worthing

133

At his funeral there were many young maidens all dressed in white, one of whom read a sermon, supposedly written by Oliver. Legend says that he was buried upside down, so that on the last day when the world is turned upside down, he would be the only one the right way up. Needless to say this tale has been told of several other Sussex eccentrics.

Belloc's famous mill at Shipley in 1980

OAK APPLE DAY

Folklore can sometimes be very confusing. This is certainly so with Oak Apple Day (May 29), as the name and the customs associated with it are also often attached to Ash Wednesday. Just to confuse things even more, the day has a number of alternative names – Pinching Day, Nettle Day, Shik-Shak Day or, as many of the boys would have it, Pinch-Bum Day.

The origin is usually laid at the door of King Charles II, who, while asleep in the branches of the Boscobel Oak during his famous escape in 1651, became cramped and had to be pinched by Colonel Carless. The story was printed in a broadsheet of 1660 in anticipation of the Restoration.

Schoolboys either enjoyed or dreaded this day, as it was once a very widespread custom to receive a pinch, or a punch, if you failed to wear an oak leaf, or an oak apple. Equally unpleasant alternatives were to be stung on the legs with nettles, or to be pricked with a pin. There was even a game called Pinch Me, which was played only on this particular day in the late nineteenth century.

Many Sussex writers have commented on the customs associated with the day. Doris Hall said that the Union Flag was flown from the Ditchling School flagstaff, and pupils paraded around it and were then given a holiday. Lillian Candlin recorded that on May 29 Brighton fishermen decorated their boats with branches of oak, and the Kings Head pub in West Street was also decorated – this continuing well into Victoria's reign.

The Jacobite song *The 29th of May* was still sung in Sussex even after the dethronement of Charles II in 1668, and the tune was later used for the children's hymn, *All Things Bright and Beautiful.*

OBSTINACY

Sussex folk have always believed in the phrase 'You may push and you may shuv, but I'm hemmed if I'll be druv'. In other words a true native of the county would resolutely refuse to be persuaded to any course of action against his (or her) better judgement, or even in too much of a rush.

My grandfather was a typical Sussex man of the old school, and when anyone pointed out some job which badly needed his attention, his invariable reply was, 'I'll do it drackly', which meant anytime when it suited him.

Pig-headed was the adjective most often employed by our detractors, and the Sussex pig was often pointed out as a suitable county emblem, typified by the famous pottery pigs manufactured in Rye.

Most Sussex writers have been quick to comment on this particular aspect of the Sussex character. The Reverend Coker-Egerton, Rector of Burwash, told of a freezing morning when one of his parishioners overtook a boy in a cart, sitting hunched up and appearing to be thoroughly cold and miserable. He was unwise enough to offer the advice, 'If I were you, my little man, I'd get down and walk'. The reply was, 'No, that I wunt. Not if I freezes fust'.

When Tom Neeves, a village carpenter, painted the Ten Commandments for Udimore Church, the vicar quite reasonably pointed out that he had accomplished only eight. The typical reply was, 'Ah well, I rackon thems as many as what you'll kip'.

As well as his OBSTINACY, the Sussex man always liked to have the last word. When a labourer went to a doctor's house to have a tooth pulled, he was asked which tooth was to come out. This was during the hard times of the early 1800s, and the man replied dourly, 'Oh, any one yer like, Sor. I aint perticular, as there aint nothin' for any o' em to do.'

PLACE RHYMES

A very large collection of rhymes about villages and towns in Sussex can be assembled. Here are just a few of the more interesting ones, in alphabetical order.

Amberley

> *Amberley - God knows*
> *All among the rooks and crows*
> *Where the good potato grows.*

Amberley natives were sometimes said to be either web-footed, or yellow-bellied. The village was sometimes referred to as 'Amberley God Knows'.

Arundel

> *Since William rose and Harold fell.*
> *There have been Earls of Arundel.*
> *And Earls old Arundel shall have*
> *Whilst rivers flow and forests wave.*

Buxted

> *Master Huggett and his man John.*
> *They did cast the first cannon.*

Ralph Hogg was a sixteenth century iron founder, who had as his assistant John Johnson.

Brighton

> *Brighton is a pretty place,*
> *Worthing is much taken.*
> *If you can't get any other meat,*
> *There's hogsflesh and bacon.*

Please do not ask me to explain that one.

Berwick

The parson was poor and so were the people,
So they sold the bells to repair the steeple.
Or ever they'd be left in the lurch,
They'd sell the steeple to repair the church.

The story from Berwick is that the steeple was in need of repair, so they sacrificed some of their bells, which were sold to Alfriston. To make up the deficiency, they bought a small ship's bell from a wreck. Jevington has a similar rhyme.

Chichester

If Chichester church steeple fall,
In England there's no King at all.

When the steeple actually fell in 1861, Queen Victoria was on the throne.

Firle

When Firle Beacon wears a cap,
We in the valley gets a drap.
When Firle Beacon's head is bare.
All next day it will be fair.

One of many weather rhymes associated with places. There are similar ditties connected with Alfriston, Wolstonbury, and Chanctonbury Ring.

Heathfield

Heathfield for poor men, Warbleton for slaves.
Brightling for rich men, Dallington for knaves.

Horsham

Horsham is a funny place, and holds some funny people.
One very funny thing it has, and that's a crooked steeple.
The Town Hall too is queerly placed, in a rather funny quarter.
One side always blows a Gale, the other stands Attwater.

And so on for twelve more verses. Gale and Attwater were two shopkeepers, near the Town Hall.

Northiam

O rare Norgem, thou dost far exceed.
Beckley, Peasemarsh, Udimore and Brede.

'Norgem' is the dialect form of Northiam.

Piddinghoe

Englishmen fight, Frenchmen too.
We doant, we live in Pidd'nhoo.

Apparently the people of this village considered themselves much superior to the 'English'.

Pevensey

I wish with all my heart, Napoleon Bonaparte,
Would land on Pevensey Level.
We'd meet him there, and fight him square.
And send him to the Devil.

One of several rhymes from the time of warfare with the French.

Rudgwick

Rugick (Rudgwick) for riches,
Green (Wisborough Green) for poors,
Billingshurst for pretty girls,
Horsham for whores.

Rottingdean

> *Rottingdean boys, Rottingdean boys,*
> *Eyes like diamonds, teeth like pearles.*
> *Laced up boots and corduroys,*
> *You cannot better those Rottingdean boys.*

Thakeham

> *Thakeham boys are bulldogs,*
> *Nutbourne boys are brave.*
> *But little boys of Chiltington (West Chiltington),*
> *Will tear them all to rags.*

Warnham

> *Warnham once, Rusper twice.*
> *Rugick three times over.*
> *When the old cock crows, everybody knows,*
> *That it gives you warning.*

This was given to me as a rhyme for a 'he' game.

PROPHECIES

ALTHOUGH we cannot claim an Old Mother Shipton in Sussex folklore, country folk were not unwilling to use many everyday items to help them see into the future. Many wise women were adept at reading the tea-leaves, and even for those who didn't share this gift, there were some simple beliefs associated with a 'stranger', the name for a stalk of tea floating in the cup. This could be placed on the back of the hand, and hit with the other hand. The number of smacks before the stranger moves will foretell the number of days before a visitor will arrive. If after the tea has been made, the tea pot lid is left off, this is also a sure sign of a stranger coming.

A nice portent to ensure that new neighbours will never want, is to give them a basket of eggs.

A child born on a Sunday will not drown or be hanged. Those born at three, six, nine or twelve will see much that is hidden from others.

Less pleasant were death portents. A rattling of the church door meant that it would be opened before the end of the week to receive a coffin. If a corpse failed to stiffen after death, it meant that another member of the same family would soon die.

Almost any common everyday thing could be used to foretell the future, but for a real prophecy we must go to Twineham, where it was believed that at the end of the world, the first people to awake from the dead will be the favoured folk of that village.

PUB GAMES

THE village inn was a place providing refreshment and entertainment, although both were aimed very largely at the male section of the community. The inn depended on its customers for its existence, as an old song said:

> *If it wasn't for us poor labouring men,*
> *What would the publican do?*
> *For the men buy baccy and the women buy gin,*
> *And so the game goes on.*
> *If it wasn't for us poor labouring men,*
> *What would the publican do?*

Drink was very cheap by modern standards, but we have to remember that the farm labourer probably earned less than a pound a week, and out of this he had to keep a family. As well as the drink and food, many publicans tried to provide as much simple entertainment as possible; although most of this has now disappeared, to be replaced by more sophisticated forms.

A century or so ago games available in the average village pub might include ring-the-bull, toad-in-the-hole, shove-ha'penny, and a table for card games. The game of ring-the-bull or ringing-the-bull was not too difficult, and there were no rules. Getting the ring over the hook more times than your opponent was all that mattered. Sometimes a simple hook would be replaced by something more elaborate, such as the stuffed head of an animal. The ring was a bull's nose-ring, on a six foot cord, suspended about four feet away from the hook. There were many different techniques. Bob Copper, in his book *Early to Rise,* speaks of a man who turned his back and sent the ring towards the big old clock in the corner, yet by some feat of magic the ring would change its orbit and end up neatly on the hook.

Toad-in-the-hole is much more complicated, and a nice example was shown to me in Horsham Museum. About the size of a tea trolley, the top includes a number of holes, a wheel and a metal toad. Metal discs are thrown into the holes and thence down into numbered sections. The toad's mouth must have been the equivalent of a bulls-eye.

A simpler version consists of a box standing about twenty inches from the floor, with a single round hole into which a metal disc or coin is thrown. I have been told that originally George III threepenny-pieces, which weighed exactly two ounces, were used. Sometimes the discs provided had the name of the pub printed on them. There are toad-in-the-hole games at the Lewes Arms, and the Ram Inn at Firle, and no doubt there are others.

Another popular game was shove-ha'penny, supposed to have been derived from the game of shovel-board of Elizabethan days. Although there are some very large shove-ha'penny boards, most are about the size of a modern bagatelle board. The game is played with brass discs, about the size of an old halfpenny. The board I remember from my childhood was probably typical. It had a well polished hardwood surface, with lines across, dividing it into nine beds. Two parallel lines marked the extent of the playing area. Five half-pennies were used, and two people or two teams could play. The players placed the discs slightly overlapping the edge of the front of the board, striking them with the palm. Each bed should score no more than three (a full house). More than that counted to the opposite team.

Spinning jenny at the George and Dragon, Burpham

Possibly most rare of these old pub games is the spinning jenny, or twizzler, mounted on the ceiling. This consists of a large revolving pointer, and some kind of dial. Several reasons are advanced for the true use of these fascinating items of equipment. One is that they were used to decide who should buy the next round of drinks, or they may have been used for a definite game. The pubs that still have them usually claim that they were used by the smuggling fraternity to divide their contraband. Certainly smuggling was widespread in Sussex, with many gangs using an inn as their headquarters. At Burpham the George and Dragon has an example of a typical spinning jenny, as also has the Spotted Cow at

Angmering. In the *Petworth Magazine* of December 1998, Janet Austin mentions a spinning jenny (also referred to as a smugglers clock) in the Foresters Arms in Kirdford, and the editor of the magazine appends a note that a similar device is described by Gertrude Jekyll in her book *Old West Surrey* (1904).

Among card players, cribbage seems to have been the most often played game. It was undoubtedly my grandfather's favourite game, although as he got older he had difficulty in finding an opponent who knew how to play it. Crib was the affectionate name used by the players of a game which was said to have been invented long ago by Sir John Suckling. The score is kept by little wooden pegs (or even matchsticks) which are placed in holes down each side of the cribbage board.

A game once very popular in pubs (and elsewhere) was up-Jenkins (alternative names were tippet and spoof). A typical game began with two teams on either side of a table, one side having sixpence hidden in one player's hand. The other team's captain gave the orders, and no-one obeyed an order unless it came from the captain. The first order was 'up Jenkins', with the hands coming up as clenched fists. Then followed 'elephant gate openers' (opening and shutting hands), 'creepy crawlies' (scrabbling on the table), 'butterflies' (hands waving about), 'lobster pots' (fingers dancing on table), and finally 'smashoms' (all hands crash down on the table). The whole point was to decide who held the sixpence, and the captain then ordered all hands to be removed except the one which he had decided held the coin. If he was correct, then the team with the sixpence handed it over to the opposing side, and if not they kept it for another round. It all sounds rather tame, but probably it was more fun than a mere description can convey.

RAILWAYS

SOME day someone should write a book on Sussex railway folklore, but until that time, here are a selection of items which might appear in such a volume.

A close-knit group of men, working together, are bound to throw up annual customs. Horsham Goods Yard, in the days when it was a busy, noisy place, had a New Year's Eve custom recalled by my wife, whose father and brother were both railwaymen. Just prior to midnight, fog signals would be placed on the rails near the signal box in the yard. Many were used, placed about twenty-five yards apart. As the midnight hour approached, a driver would take an engine speeding towards the road bridge, exploding each one as he went. The sounds could be heard all over the town, and every year there were complaints, which somehow were forgotten when the next year came around. Like many annual customs it ceased at the time of the Second World War.

Children contributed to railway lore. If you threw a coin on an engine, and it stayed on, this meant good luck. However it was always unlucky to walk under a rail bridge when a train was passing on top. If you have to do this, then cross your fingers and do not speak. To see the last two carriages or trucks of a train was considered bad luck, but to see two engines meant just the opposite.

Trains often had affectionate or derisory nicknames. 'The Linger and Die' (or more complimentary, 'The Horsham Flyer') were the names for the branch line (and train) from Horsham to Brighton. 'The Selsey Bumper' was the name for the Hundred of Manhood and Selsey Tramway. A song called this train the 'Sidlesham Snail'. The drivers kept a pile of stones in the cab to throw at rabbits or game birds. 'Daddy Long Legs' was the descriptive name for the extension of Volk's Electric Railway at Brighton. 'The Lancing Belle' was the name for a special train from Brighton, run each day during the 1960s strike, for the benefit of the workmen at Lancing Carriage Works.

Some names were inspired by the railway's initials. London, Brighton and South Coast Railway (LB and SCR) could be interpreted as 'Ladies Boots and Shoes Carefully Repaired'. South Eastern and Chatham (SE and C) was appropriately rendered as 'Slow, Easy and Comfortable'.

Here are two rhymes, the first from my own childhood.

Teddy on the railway, picking up stones.
Along came an engine, and broke Teddy's bones.
Oh said Teddy 'That's not fair'.
'Oh' said the engine, 'I don't care'.

This one was from the Brighton Locomotive Works:

God made the bees,
The bees make honey.
Peaky does the work,
And the gang gets the money.

Peaky was Arthur Peake, a popular chargeman.

There were scores of stories and near-legends connected with Sussex railways. Aristocratic passengers in the early days were allowed to stay in their own carriages, which were driven on to flat trucks at the rear of the train. This practice gave rise to many stories of such passengers having their trucks disconnected in tunnels, and being left stranded in the darkness.

The Dyke Railway had its own peculiar rules. An electric bell rang on the Dyke Golf Course when the train was about to start, to encourage intending passengers to drink up. One morning the first train was returning to Brighton, and it met a large horse on the line. Whistling made no impression on the beast, and even the fireman waving his arms had no effect. Finally the train had to proceed slowly on its way with the horse leading the way.

The trains on the Horsham-Brighton branch passed close to Horsham Cricket Ground, and the drivers would slow down so that they could note the latest scores to pass on to their colleagues on their arrival at Brighton. There was a time when trains were known for their spot-on time-keeping. A contributor to the *West Sussex Gazette* in 1981 said that his grandfather went to a particular spot where he could see the Midhurst to Pulborough train pass, so that he could set his watch right for the day. A mother always remembered at what time her first child was born, as the six o'clock milk train was just entering the local station. But things other than time-keeping were not always so predictable. The early railway station at Burgess Hill had a portable platform, which was moved into position according to where the driver decided to stop his train.

And lastly, some supernatural happenings on the railways. The well-known rail tunnel at Balcombe featured in a ghost story which appeared in the magazine *Soldier* in March 1961. Mr Myer, who had been a sentry on duty at the entrance to the tunnel early in the Second World War, told of a ghostly experience one night. A number of German bombs fell close by, and he took refuge in the tunnel. After a few minutes he saw three men approaching, and he challenged them, but they then grew faint and vanished. When he told the story next day to a foreman platelayer, he was informed that during the First World War, three soldiers who had been on sentry duty at the same spot, were run down by a train and killed.

Clayton Tunnel, which has an entrance like a Sussex castle, was built in this fashion as Sussex folk were said to be afraid of tunnels, and the castle-like exterior was supposed to make it more user-friendly. Behind the 'castle' facade was Tunnel House, a property originally intended as the railway wages office during the building of the tunnel in 1836, In 1841 it became a railwayman's cottage. Apart from the sound of trains hurtling along underneath, the residents also had to cope with the two ghosts, said to be Charlie, and the White Lady – both of whom had been killed on the track below.

The railway tunnel at Clayton

RIDDLES

OUR Sussex ancestors loved riddles, some very simple and some most complex. Here are just a few from the many I have collected over the years.

First some connected with Sussex places:

> *Why is Crawley the longest place in the world?*
> *Because the Sun is at one end and the Half Moon at the other.*

> *Where was beer sold by the pound?*
> *At Bury.*

Nancy Green sold beer from a shop on the Common close to the village pound.

> *Where do they shoe their magpies?*
> *Piddinghoe.*

The magpies were black and white oxen.

> *Why is going up St Luke's Lane in Newhaven like*
> *going up to bed?*
> *Because there are Bannisters on either side.*

Bannisters were Newhaven furniture shops.

> *What are three lies and all true?*
> *Hellingly, Chiddingly and Hoathly.*

Other Sussex place names ending in 'ly' can be substituted. The Sussex pronunciation for the end of these place names was always like the word lie.

George Belton had several good riddles, but not always the answers to go with them. This is a typical one.

Two men with horse teams met. One said 'You got a long team this morning'. The other said 'Yes – if you gave me one of your horses, I should have twice as many as you'. 'Maybe,' said the first, 'But if you gave me one of yours, we should both have the same'. How many horses were there in each team?'.

Another complex one, but at least I can provide the answer.

Two legs sat on Three legs, with one leg upon his lap. Along came Four legs and ran away with one leg. Up jumps Two legs and throws Three legs at Four legs, to make Four legs bring back one leg.

What are we talking about? A man is sitting on a milking stool with a leg of lamb on his lap. A dog steals the lamb, and the man throws the stool at it to make it bring it back.

A charming one from Ethel Powell, who had it from her grandfather.

Three fourths of a cross, and a circle complete. Two semi-circles, perpendicular do meet. And a triangle that stands on two feet. Two semi-circles and a circle complete. What is it?'

The answer is Tobacco.
And finally a very slightly naughty one.

Open like a barn door, shut up like a trap. You can guess a thousand things, and never think of that.

Knee-length knickers, with an opening down the back.

ROUGH MUSIC

ROUGH Music, or to use a more ancient term, Skymington, was the group response of local residents to one of their number who had misbehaved. If the law could not be invoked, or was inappropriate, then this form of mob justice was the last resort. The usual manner was for a crowd to assemble after dark, outside the house of the offender. Many would be equipped with kitchen utensils and make-shift musical instruments, in fact anything that would make a discordant noise. The demonstration would go on for a considerable time, and would probably not be confined to just one night. The effect on those within can only be imagined, but it must have been extremely frightening, as the din was combined with much shouting and threatening behaviour.

The last time Rough Music took place in Sussex is uncertain, but we hear of examples in West Hoathly as recently as 1947 and 1952, also in relatively modern times at Turners Hill and Graffham. In the nineteenth century many eruptions of Rough Music were noted by the Sussex press – here are just two typical examples:

In 1861 large numbers assembled outside the house of a Mr Kerby, at Chichester, shouting and hooting, and even smashing windows. The police were called, but their efforts were not very successful, and the following day the mayor arranged for notices in the streets pointing out that such disturbances were unlawful. This seemed to have little effect, as that night the trouble re-commenced, until the police arrested one of the ringleaders.

In 1863 King Street, Arundel, was the scene of similar demonstrations in front of the house of a man who, it was said, had badly beaten his wife. The ill-treatment of wives, and children, was one of the most common reasons for such demonstrations.

This is a genuine folk custom which seemed to die slowly, perhaps because sometimes there appeared to be no satisfactory substitute. A woman brought up in Petworth told me her recollection of seeing a group of 'rough musicians' coming out one night. Her mother realising what was about to happen, sent her daughter to bed and forbade her to even peep out of the window.

But as one man remarked: 'There's no fun in Rough Music, unless the person concerned will come out'.

SAINT LEONARD AND HIS FOREST

SUPERIOR folk will tell you that St Leonard never visited Sussex, but he gave his name to a part of the Wealden woodland north of Horsham, which even today is famous for its folklore and legends. Once the forest was much larger, part of Anderida described by the Venerable Bede in 731 as 'thick and inaccessible, a place of retreat for the large herds of deer, wolves and wild boars'.

Probably the best known of the St Leonard's Forest legends concerns the dragons. The first is almost certainly allegorical, as it includes St Leonard himself, who is said to have fought the beast in the depths of the forest, and in proof of this the lily of the valley beds are always mentioned, as each flower is supposed to represent a drop of the saint's blood spilt in the conflict. (Sometimes it is snowdrops rather than lilies, and even the dragon's blood instead of the saint's). Hard facts are difficult to come by, but there was said to have been a chapel in or near the forest dedicated to St Leonard, first noted in 1320 but in ruins by 1637. At a Crawley exhibition in 1865 an old key was on show, which was said to have been from the chapel, and had been discovered in the drained moat of Bewbush Manor.

Road through St Leonard's Forest, early in the last century

151

The second dragon story is much better documented, as it appears in an account published in London in 1614. The tale has a marvellous title which begins 'True and Wonderful. A discourse relating a strange and monstrous serpent or dragon lately discovered and yet living by his strong and violent poyson'. It goes on to tell of this dragon living 'two miles from Horsam, in a woode called St. Leonard's Forrest'. The beast was said to be nine feet in length, and with scales along its back. On either side it had great bunches which it was conjectured would in time grow into wings (presumably this was a young dragon). The venom of the beast was the cause of death of several people and animals. A number of witnesses were mentioned, including the Horsham carrier John Steele, and a widow woman. A saying attributed to St Leonard is that in his forest 'no nightingales should sing, or adders sting'; but he didn't actually mention dragons.

St Leonard's Forest dragon stories refuse to die, and a radio broadcast in 1991 spoke of 1,600 sightings in the previous twenty years.

Another very well known forest legend concerns Mick Miles (or Mike Mills) who was a smuggler, and who agreed to race with the Devil, for the ultimate possession of the smuggler's soul. The mile long avenue where the two of them raced is still pointed out today, and Mick fell down dead at the moment of victory, a winner by a quarter of a mile. There are several different versions of this story, but the most telling ending is that from the time of the race nothing has grown along the route.

Captain William Powlett (known as Squire Powlett) lived in the forest in the reign of George I. He died in 1746, and his grave and monument are in West Grinstead's church. For reasons unknown his ghost appears in the forest, headless, and leaping upon the backs of horses being ridden after dark. Motorists and cyclists in modern times appear to be untroubled, but a woman at one of my talks said her husband had seen a headless figure in the forest on All Souls Day. She said she had not previously heard the story of the headless horseman.

Richard Gates, an illiterate elderly man, living in the forest, claimed that King Charles II hid in a yew tree, and 'an ol' woman came out and gave him some peas puddn'. (The village of Pease Pottage is not far away). This account was quoted by Marjorie Baldwin in her book on St Leonard's Forest; she suggested that this could have been during the King's flight to Brighton, and that a tree stood in front of Yew Tree Cottage, but had been cut down a long time ago.

Another story says that the King hid in Sun Oak, the finest tree in the forest, named for it's shape, and once the meeting place of the Crawley and Horsham Hunt.

Still another well known story, of slightly more modern times, concerns the 'Black Princess' – in fact Helena Bennett, an Indian woman who lived in the forest alone and neglected for more than half a century. She had been the wife of a French soldier, General de Boigne, who subsequently left her and married a French woman. Helena, remained a lonely figure, spoken of also as 'the black woman'. Her grave may still be seen at the entrance to Horsham churchyard, at one time enclosed by iron railings, later removed.

Tomb of the 'Black Princess' in Horsham parish churchyard

A Horsham headmaster told me of how a group of his older boys decided to spend a night in St Leonard's Forest with cameras and recording gear, but for reasons which they were unwilling to discuss they departed hurriedly, leaving their expensive equipment to be collected the following day. So perhaps the old stories still make sense.

SNAKES

IT seems that Sussex was once a county noted for its snakes. A ballad of 1652 has the lines 'Here's no Sussex serpent to fright you in my bundle'. Sometimes snakes were confused with dragons, in fact the two names seemed to be interchangeable.

Stories of large snakes were not uncommon. The *West Sussex Gazette* in 1863 reported a monster snake seen at Warningcamp. This was at least eight feet in length, with its girth being greatly in excess of what would be proportionate. A crusade against the creature was organised.

From Fittleworth, Charlotte Latham wrote in 1868 of 'an oudacious large snake' in that neighbourhood. Its lair was near a path, and it would not allow anyone to pass it, rushing out with a terrible hissing sound and a very bad smell.

WH Hudson, in his book *Nature in Downland* (1900), tells a strange story of a big snake found by boys on the Downs between Jevington and Willingdon. The lads found this creature coiled up, and were considerably frightened on account of its great size and threatening aspect, as it rose up hissing loudly at them. Its movements were slow as it was hindered by 'a quantity of thickness in the middle'. Arming themselves with big flints, they began to stone it, and one sharp flint cut its body open and from the wound fell a full grown lark. When it was dead, four other birds were forced out. They took the snake home and hung it on a branch of a tree, and when the schoolmaster measured it he found it was exactly four feet long. Hudson commented that there was nothing incredible in the story, as he knew of much bigger snakes killed in this country.

Most snake stories concern adders, which according to Hudson could be tamed very easily after a few days in captivity. Adders are said to be deaf, and legend says that if the marks on its belly could be understood they would say 'If I could only hear as well as see, no mortal man should master me'. Fat from behind the head of the adder was highly valued, but it took six dead adders to provide enough oil to fill a small bottle. George Attrill of Fittleworth had his own bottle of adder oil, which he told me was good for ear-ache, bites, rheumatism, a thorn in the eye, and many other complaints.

The usual rate for catching adders was sixpence each, quite a princely sum for the times, and adder hunts were organised in several villages. Once the chemist in Uckfield sold the oil as a certain cure for deafness.

A strange belief existed that young adders will run into the mother's mouth at a sign of danger. Another singular idea was that adders (or in fact any snake) though cut in two, cannot die until the sun sets.

Holed stones (always considered lucky in Sussex) were sometimes known as snake stones and hung on cattle to keep adders away.

Snakes have always been considered unlucky in Sussex, and even as recently as 1936 the erection of a likeness of a serpent at the Queen Victoria Hospital, East Grinstead, was very unpopular. However it had to remain, as protesters were told it would cost £63 to remove it.

George Attrill of Fittleworth n 1955.
He showed me his bottle of adder oil
(taken from adders e had killed)
which was his 'cure-all'

155

TIPTEERS

AROUND Christmas time, the mummers (or tipteers, as they were called in Sussex), came out with their 'Death and Resurrection' plays. The male actors played the same characters year after year, until perhaps their sons took over on the death of their fathers. The texts were not committed to paper, and as with folk songs were subject to variations through the years. The age of the plays causes some disagreement, but we have the character of the Turkish Knight in many of the plays, to link the action with the Crusades. Other characters were King George (or sometimes Saint George), Old Father Christmas, Beelzebub and the Doctor. Costumes were basic, often merely old clothes with pieces of bright cloth sewn on, and faces were almost certainly blacked, until around the nineteenth century. In retrospect it is easy to see old traditions such as the tipteering plays continuing in an unbroken thread through the years. In fact there were probably times when the tradition was broken for various reasons, only to be resumed again after a lapse. Nowadays we have many revival plays being performed each year, often by morris men. Looking back, we know of some groups of mummers that we think of as part of the tradition, although many of them were themselves revivals. One of these old revival teams were the Boxgrove Tipteers, who flourished in the 1930s, using a play made up of a combination of texts from East Preston and Iping. It was in 1911 that Mr Foord, a farm worker, revived the East Preston play, having been part of it as a boy. The 1914–18 war put an end to that revival, and it was in 1927 that the Boxgrove Tipteers came into existence, due largely to the efforts of RJ Sharp of Chichester, who was a fiddle player. Probably due to his influence the Boxgrove team always ended their performances with several Sussex songs, and two dances – the Sussex Bonny Breastknot, and Over the Sticks. They continued to present their play until the outbreak of the 1939 war, having taken part in a national folk dance festival in London, in 1937.

In 1961 George Attrill told me of the Fittleworth play, which he said was flourishing back in the 1890s, with a leader called Harry Puttick from Upperton. The cast consisted of Father Christmas, Billy Twing Twang, King George, The Turkish Knight, the Doctor, and The Prince of Peace. George said they played to all the big houses in Fittleworth, ending with a few pence and a drink. By the end of the evening they

The Sompting Mummers' play, Boxing Day, 1993

would be somewhat 'under the weather'. Then the 1914-18 war put a stop to this play, and it was not revived until George got a gang together for the occasion of the King's Jubilee in 1935. Following this, it was brought out on several occasions.

Most villages had their own plays. Gordon Hall recalled an uncle who played King George in the Chailey play. He brandished a rusty cutlass on his first appearance, and the barmaid in fainted. For this the mummers were evicted from the pub.

There is a delightful account of the Rottingdean Mummers in Angela Thirkell's book *Three Houses* (1931). Her grandfather was Sir Edward Burne-Jones, so the players must have tried their hardest to impress, but she recalled a group of poor labourers in smocks and leggings, with just a few pieces of coloured paper sewn on their clothes. The cast of the play *St George and the Dragon*, consisted of St George, the Turkish Knight, the Dragon, the Doctor and a very unfeminine Princess. At the end, one of the cast recited:

> *Here comes I, Little Devil Doubt.*
> *If you don't give me money, I'll kick you all out.*
> *Money I want, money I crave,*
> *If you don't give me money, I'll kick you into your grave.*

They ended by singing The Mistletoe Bough, and left, no doubt slightly richer, whilst the drawing room curtains were thrown back to let out the scent of unwashed corduroys.

Sometimes topical events were added to the story. At Sompting in 1884 St George threatened to 'chop up the Turkish Knight as small as dust, and send him to the cook-shop to be made into mincepie crust'. Apparently this referred to a libel action of 1883, by a duke against the editor of *Vanity Fair*, who had published an article stating that the duke's father was an army supplier who had put portions of dead soldiers into his casks of meat.

George Attrill said that a feature of the plays was the 'magic talk' of Father Christmas, who introduced the play. This was a mix of nonsense and riddles in Sussex dialect, such as:

> *'I saw a man wheeling a left-handed wheelbarrow,*
> *Who could not see anything without opening his eyes,*
> *And could not speak without moving his tongue'.*

Old Father Christmas usually began his opening speech with:

> *Welcome Old Father Christmas, welcome or welcome not.*
> *I hope old Father Christmas will never be forgot.*

These lines sometimes became divorced from the rest of the play, and I have come across them without any mention of the tipteers or their play.

Most mummers concluded their play with a song or carol, sometimes having no connection with the story or the season. But this was not always the case, as we have the Sussex Mummers Carol (collected by Lucy Broadwood at Lyne, near Rusper in 1889) with its very suitable lines 'O mortal men, remember well, when Christ our Lord was born'.

TOASTS

TOASTS were often brought out on convivial occasions, such as harvest suppers and other village feasts. Not that the countryman of the past really needed any excuse for drinking, but it seems that an apt toast preceding the drink. added to the enjoyment of the moment.

> *Bread when you're hungry, beer when you're dry.*
> *Bed when you're tired, and Heaven when you die.*

What more could a working man need. But in case anyone doubted his reasons for drinking, this toast makes it all clear.

> *I have several good reasons for drinking,*
> *And one has just entered my head.*
> *If a man should not drink when he's living,*
> *How the hell can he drink when he's dead.*

The Royal Oak at Barcombe, one of many pubs where old drinking customs were nurtured

George Belton of Madehurst had a toast full of good-Jnatured wishes towards the missing ladies.

> Good health to you and all the rest,
> And to the one that I love best.
> Although she's not here to take her part,
> I'll drink her health with all my heart.
> I'll drink her health in water,
> I'll drink her health in wine,
> I'll drink good health to you and your true love,
> And jolly good health to mine.

Sometimes a book full of homely philosophy was condensed into two lines:

> Here's to the bee that stung Adam.
> And set all the world a-jogging.

But discretion had to be kept in mind:

> We meet to be merry, then let us part wise.
> Nor suffer the bottle, to blind reason's eyes.

There were hundreds more, but here is a final thought:

> A shady lane, a gravel walk.
> A pretty girl, and time to talk.

TREACLE MINES

TREACLE mines are part of the vast world-wide collection of tall tales. The mines are found in many counties of England (no less than nineteen examples were mentioned in just one issue of the *Folklore Society News*). Sussex appears to have a considerable number, including sites in Faygate, Lewes, Rowhook, Polegate, and Sompting. My own childhood memory includes the mines at Faygate, which were apparently served by the 'Rusper Docks'.

Sompting Treacle Mines have their own historian, Alfred Longley, who in his book *Alexandra Terrace* (1960), tells us a lot about Jimmy Smuggles, a local character who was connected with the mines. Alfred relates how Jimmy could lower the chimney of the mine so that the harvest moon could pass without getting stuck to it. The book even includes a picture of Jimmy Smuggles, proving his existence.

In Worthing close by, a lazy person is often said to work at the Sompting Treacle Mines. At Lewes, the entrance to the mines is supposed to be through a pair of double doors in the cliff face north of the town.

Gordon Brookes has suggested that children nowadays are more likely to be interested in ice cream mines

At a talk I was asked, by a young man with a straight face, if I had heard of the Colgate Toothpaste Mines.

TUNNELS

IT HAS been said that every Sussex village has a witch, a ghost and a secret tunnel. Certainly there are tunnel tales, some fairly vague, attached to a great many Sussex villages (and towns). Inns often have tales of underground passages or rooms, and many of these are said to be connected with the smuggling trade. Many of the tunnels are supposed to end up in the church, or churchyard – and just to add a little more interest to the stories, a number have supernatural twists to them.

Additionally, many underground or hidden places in old houses were constructed to hide Roman Catholic priests in Elizabethan times. Later they were used by hunted Cavaliers, and later still by smugglers.

The following are just a few of the more interesting tunnels and passages, with some of the folklore and fancy which has inevitably become attached to them.

Arundel has many tunnel stories, perhaps because excavations are relatively easy in the largely chalk ground. One story tells of a secret room with its entrance covered by a carpet in the drawing room of the castle. From a false wall in this room there was said to be a tunnel running for an indeterminate distance. A man and his dog (some versions say the animal was a duck), set out to find the end of the tunnel, but were never seen again. Another version says that the dog emerged unscathed about five miles away, two weeks later. There is said to be a tunnel from Maltravers Street, and another under the Eagle 'big enough to hold a dray'. Another tunnel from the castle garden to Anne Howard Gardens, was later dismissed with the mundane explanation that it was actually a disused apple store.

But the best known Arundel tale is about a tunnel said to run from the Castle Keep to Amberley Castle, at least three miles away. There is a very involved account, which tells of a treasure of gold and silver plate owned by the Cavaliers, which was manhandled through the tunnel, and then taken from Amberley by pack horse to be finally buried in a deep well. A correspondent in the *West Sussex Gazette* in 1966 wrote that in 1906-8, a fellow boarder at his school told how his father took part in an attempt to send a greyhound dog from the Amberley end of the tunnel, right through to the Arundel entrance. The attempt failed, but later twenty rats were put into the tunnel, and some were recaptured at the other end.

Broadwater, adjacent to Worthing, has many stories of smuggling activity. The village had a number of underground passages, and the large tombs in the churchyard were said to be used for hiding contraband. One passage led from St Mary's Cottage to the church, and a former rector was said to have confirmed the existence of another passage between the church and the Manor House, which he presumed was connected with smuggling.

A few years ago I visited the Manor House (now a school) and found there was no apparent evidence, although there were memories of a bricked-up entrance to a possible passageway, and most people were aware of the tunnel stories. A common explanation was that when the Manor House was a monastery the monks used the passage nightly to reach the porch of the church, to help the sick and distressed.

At Crawley there is a story of an underground tunnel from the Ancient Priors in the High Street, to the former Franciscan monastery. However the monastery was built on farmland only in 1861, and no story of a tunnel has ever been connected with this building. There may be a tunnel connected with the Ancient Priors, but it is unlikely that it ever went to the friary. Smugglers are more likely to be the instigators, as a woman who lived at Ancient Priors as a child recalled a secret panel between it and the house next door, said to have been used by the smugglers. I was once shown a similar secret aperture between the old Prince of Wales inn in West Street, Horsham, and the next door building.

A cottage in Easebourne was being modernised in 1963, and a book dated 1602 was discovered, grey with dust, entitled *A Little Memorial. The right and proper use of the Sacraments*. This had been written by a Spanish priest, Father Arias, possibly one of the priests who visited Cowdray during penal times. A chimney-like structure in the cottage may have been the hiding place for travelling priests. The man who found this curiosity said: 'It had three sides like a chimney, but didn't go up through the roof. I suppose a man could have hidden there, and there might once have been a panel in front of it, but it would have been a very tight squeeze'. A woman at one of my talks told me of a tunnel from Easebourne Priory to Cowdray, and another from a pub in Easebourne which was used by smugglers.

The 'Catecombs' at Goodwood, described as 'stone cells underground, which are as well contrived as curious' were created by the Second Duke of Richmond to house his menagerie, one of the noted features of the estate in the eighteenth century. The Duke died in 1750 and his zoo evidently died with him, although in 1911 some of the passages still remained, and even 80 years later the site was still discernable.

In Horsham there was a story of tunnels on the north side of Pondtail Road at the junction with Warnham Road. The owner of the big house there said (in the late 1960s) that there were three tunnels, brick-lined and high enough to walk through. The first went from the house to the old Dog and Bacon (next to the present pub). The second went to the larger house on the north side of Wimblehurst Road. The third went to the edge of Warnham Pond. Rex Godliman, who told me these stories in 1995, added that he had also mentioned them in more recent times to a woman who had lived in West Parade nearby for many years, and she confirmed them.

Horsham's best known tunnel is in Springfield Road, and came to light in modern times when the gas works site was being cleared. It was a Sunday morning in 1959 when a group of us visited the tunnel which had been discovered leading from a cellar by a workman. The passageway, which was well built and dry, ran for seventy-two feet, where it was blocked. Locals were not surprised, as tales of a tunnel which ran under the road and emerged on the opposite side in fields, were well known. Evidently the tunnel had been made to enable the Allen brothers, who had a malthouse on the site, to remove malt on which duty had not been paid. The full story of the Allen's ill-gotten malt empire is told in William Albery's *A Millenium of Facts in the History of Horsham and Sussex* (1947).

Not exactly a tunnel, but a 'black hole' existed beneath Horsham's Town Hall, reached by steps from the street. Henry Burstow said he had seen prisoners given a shove down into the miserable place, where they remained visible to the public through iron bars. Compassionate passers-by would give them tobacco or cake, and children were encouraged to give them titbits, rather like feeding zoo animals. This went on until 1846, when a new police station was built in East Street

Horsham has several other tunnel stories, but we must pass on to Rottingdean, which was a hotbed of smuggling in the eighteenth and nineteenth centuries. It was stated that half of the villagers were implicated by some means or another. Many of the smugglers' cargoes were stored in caves in the cliff face, and then taken through underground passages under the High Street. Challoners was said to be the oldest house in the village, and it has secret passages leading from the cellars down to the beach, although these are now largely blocked. Most histories of the village contain accounts of such tunnels. Another property, Down House, was said to be full of tunnels and hiding places. When workmen were digging foundations for a new squash court in the 1920s, they revealed a circular chamber nine feet in diameter, with passages – one leading to the house, and another towards Challoners.

Lastly (although one could go on and on), Worthing has its own 'grotto' and tunnel in the garden of a house in the town. When I visited it, the day was dark and dreary and the whole thing looked very forbidding, but on a summer's day I imagine it would be much more inviting. It was in the nineteenth century that James Bateman, who built Biddulph Grange in Staffordshire, came to live on the Sussex coast, and recreated a miniature Biddulph in the garden of his retirement home, in Farncombe Road, Worthing.

WARTS AND WHITLOWS

MY grandmother on my mother's side had a reputation in the family as a wise woman, one who told fortunes in the tea leaves; delineated character by hand-writing; and probably most useful of all, charmed warts away by rubbing them with a piece of raw beef, and then consigning this to the depths of the outside privy. Most charmers buried the meat in the ground.

Charms and cures for warts were legion, and were most often practised by elderly women who had a reputation for certain powers greater than normal. In other words white witches or wise women. The methods employed varied a great deal, and could involve the use of raw potato, the sap of many plants, cobwebs, adder oil, elderberry juice, and bean shells. The charm recited when using the latter went like this:

> *As this bean shell rots away,*
> *So my wart shall soon decay.*

Methods used could include pricking the wart with a pin, and sticking the pins into an ash tree; cutting notches to the total of the warts, on a stick; impaling a slug on a thorn, so that as the slug shrivelled and died the wart also declined; and (most commonly) wishing them on to another, or selling them.

Many villages had their own charmer, such as Kate Jones of Plaistow, who was renowned as a wart curer – although she had no special recipe, she just said they would disappear, and they did. Lewes in the 1880s had shop in Malling Street run by Janet Steer. She counted the patient's warts, and then bought them for a halfpenny. She said she would lose her power if she gained more than that by it.

A cure for those who suffered with a painful whitlow was to place a large black slug on a piece of clean rag, and stab it all over with a needle. The affected finger was then wrapped in the rag. Another remedy (this one offered by a Sussex gypsy), was to push a hot poker into the ground, withdraw it and then push your finger into the hole for a few minutes.

WEATHER

SINCE the beginning of time man has attempted to predict the weather. Sometimes the methods used have a good scientific basis, whilst others are completely illogical. Sussex folk were no exception, and here are just a tiny selection of the many hundreds of weather signs employed in our county.

Signs of rain to come include marigolds shutting after seven in the evening; pigs running about with straw in their mouths; cows lying down; cats lying on the back of their heads, or washing over their ears nine times; leaves of potatoes turning over; and owls screeching. At Brighton the sound of 'raking' on the beach was a sure sign of rain to come.

Signs of fine weather include spiders working during rain – the more active the spiders are, then the finer the weather will be; gnats flying in the evening. Birds were also reliable weather forecasters – a rhyme went:

> *If rooks build high,*
> *Then summer will be dry.*

Very windy and rough weather is preceded by pigs becoming restless, or the sight of porpoises off the south coast. If a moon changes on a Saturday, it always means bad weather:

> *A Saturday's moon,*
> *If it comes once in seven years,*
> *It comes too soon.*

or

> *Saturday's new,*
> *Sundays full,*
> *Always wet,*
> *And always will.*

Other common weather signs were included in these rhymes:

> *Hail brings frost to its tail.*

or

> When the swallows fly high,
> It will be dry.
> If they fly low,
> Rain water may flow.

and very usefully:

> You may safely shear your sheep,
> When the elder blossoms peep.

Days and seasons all had their own signs and rhymes:

> If Candlemas Day be fair and bright,
> Winter will have another flight.
> If Candlemas Day be cloud and rain,
> Winter will go and not come again

Most people know that one, and also the following:

> If it rains on St Swithun's Day, it will rain for forty days.

My father always told us:

> Balcony Christmas, Fireside Easter.

and he was usually correct. But how can logic come into this one:

> If Christmas Day comes on a Thursday,
> we will have a cold spring, but a warm summer.

Some were particularly depressing, such as:

> If New Years Day be summerly gay,
> 'twill be wintry weather till the first of May.

Apparently we always have to pay for good weather when it comes too early; for instance:

> January spring, not worth a pin.

February has always been noted for rain:

February fill the dyke (ditch),
Every day black or white.

My mother's dictum used to be:

As the days lengthen, so the cold strengthens.

March may make us think of the spring, but it could be very deceptive:

If March comes in like a lamb, it will go out like a lion.

But then we must remember that

March dust is worth a guinea a bushel.

April could also be uncertain

If it thunders in April,
It will thunder all summer.
But thunder on April Fools Day,
Brings much corn and hay.

However

Snow in April, means that the gates have been left open at Crowborough Fair.

This brings us to weather signs associated with actual places in Sussex. Horsham had several interesting ones. The first concerned the Town Hall clock, which if it could be heard on the edges of the town, meant rough weather. Another even weirder belief was that the weather could be forecast by whether Agate's timber yard crane had its jib lying on the ground, or left high in the air (the latter position meant fine weather). However I have been told that the crane was so unstable, that it was usual to put the jib down whenever windy weather was anticipated. Then there was the belief that a strong wind across the Carfax in the middle of the town, meant that the Toll Gate at the Star Inn in Roffey had been left open.

Perhaps more reliable were the many rhymes associated with 'caps' and 'draps' on the South Downs. Cap stands for cloud, and drap for rain). For instance:

> *When Wolstonbury has a cap,*
> *Then Hurstpierpoint will have a drap.*
> *When Beddingham Hills wears a cap,*
> *Ripe and Chalvington gets a drap.*

Similarly:

> *When the Downs stand clear, then rain is near.*
> *When the Isle of Wight is seen above the line,*
> *Brighton loses weather fine.*

There is a similar saying for Selsey Bill.

One could go on and on, but one saying which refuses to disappear is the remark that 'it looks black over Will's mothers'. Nobody seems to know who Will was, or exactly where his mother lived, but most older Sussex folk are very familiar with these two people. But I have to admit that they are not just Sussex characters, as in Lancashire they speak of 'Bill's mother', and I believe the saying is also common in other parts of the country

To conclude here is a very complete rhyme concerning St Paul's Day (January 25th):

> *If St Paul's Day be fair and clear,*
> *We'll have good luck throughout the year.*
> *If it chance to snow or rain,*
> *Then will be dear all kinds of grain.*
> *If clouds or mist darken the sky,*
> *Great stores of birds and beasts will die.*

WIFE SELLING

WIFE selling belongs not only in the world of folklore, but in literature. Thomas Hardy, in *The Mayor of Casterbridge*, tells us of a sailor buying Mrs Henchard for five guineas. The first recorded account of wife selling in England was in 1703, and the last in 1972.

In Sussex there are several examples which can be mentioned. In November 1790 a woman was sold at Ninfield for half a pint of gin, and she was reported as being 'highly delighted'. As was the custom, her husband handed her over with a halter around her neck. Later (perhaps when they had all sobered up) the original husband repurchased his wife – we are told at 'an advanced price'.

In 1797 a blacksmith at Cliffe, Lewes, sold his wife in the market for an undisclosed sum. Two years later at Brighton, a man named Staines sold his spouse for five shillings and eight pots of beer, to one James Marten.

Old Henry Burstow of Horsham in his published Reminiscences, devotes some space to the custom, mentioning three occasions when wives were sold in Horsham Market with halters round their

Horsham Market where once wives were sold

necks. About 1820 a woman named Smart was sold for three shillings and sixpence. The purchaser was a Mr Steere, and she went to live with him in Billingshurst.

At the November Fair in Horsham 1825, a blacksmith exhibited his wife for sale. She was reportedly good looking, and sold for Two Pounds, five shillings. (Notice the inflation). In 1844 Ann Holland (known as Pin-Toe Nanny) was sold for the cut price of one Pound, ten shillings, to a man named Johnson from Shipley, but he had to sell his watch in order to pay for her. Social habits were evidently changing, for the transaction was accompanied by hisses and boos from the crowd. This lady lived with her new husband for a year, during which time she bore him a child. She then ran away, finally marrying again to a man named Jim Smith.

In 1898 there were apparently a spate of wife sales in Yapton - or two at least. At the end of the Harvest, a man sold his wife to a stranger for three shillings, and the same year at the 'Shoulder of Mutton' inn, a thatcher named Marley sold his wife to a rat catcher named White for seven shillings and sixpence and a quart of beer.

Possibly the most unusual sale of a wife was by a Brighton man, who having bought himself a woman, after her death, sold her corpse to the Resurrection Men and retained her coffin as his sideboard.

The most expensive wife I have noted was sold by a man known as Pontius Pilate, (real name Humphrey), in Lewes Market for an annuity of £50.

Most likely these wife sales were in many cases, undertaken partly in jest and almost certainly while the participants were under the influence of drink. Certainly many took place in public houses, although the more serious examples were probably the ones which happened in local markets.

BIBLIOGRAPHY AND REFERENCES

Albery, William: *A Millennium of facts in the History of Horsham and Sussex 947-1947*, 1947, 1990.

Andrews, Colin: *Shepherd of the Downs*, 1979.

Axon, William EA: *Bygone Sussex*, 1897.

Baldwin, Marjorie: *The Story of the Forest*, 1971.

Beckett, Arthur: *The Spirit of the Downs*, 1909.
> *The Wonderful Weald*, 1911.
> *Adventures of a Quiet Man*, 1937.

Burke, John: *Sussex*, 1974.

Burstow, Henry: *Reminiscences of Horsham*, 1912 and 1975.

Candlin, Lillian: *Tales of Old Sussex*, 1985.
> *Memories of Old Sussex*, 1987.

Chapman, Brigid: *East Sussex Inns*, 1988.
> *West Sussex Inns*, 1988.

Cooper, Quentin and Sullivan, Paul: *Maypoles, Martyrs and Mayhem*, 1994.

Copper, Bob: *A Song for Every Season*, 1971.
> *Songs and Southern Breezes*, 1973.
> *Early to Rise*, 1976.

Crookshank, AC: St Leonard of Sussex

Davies, Roger: Tarring, 1990.

Davis, Winifred: *Lo Rare Norgam*, 1965.

Doel, G and F: *Mumming, Howling and Hoodening*, 1992.
> *Spring and Summer Customs in Sussex, Kent and Surrey*, 1995.

Egerton, J Coker: *Sussex Folk and Sussex Ways*, 1892.

Evans, AA: *On Foot in Sussex*, 1933.
> *A Saunterer in Sussex*, 1935.

Fleet, Charles: *Glimpses of Our Ancestors in Sussex*, 1882/3.

Hall, Doris: *Growing up in Ditchling*, 1985.

Hare, Augustus JC: *Sussex*, 1894.

Hare, Chris: *Historic Worthing*, 1991.

Hazlitt, WC: *Dictionary of Faiths and Folklore*, 1905.

Holmes, Eric: *Seaward Sussex*, 1920.

Hudson, WH: *Nature in Downland*, 1900.

Hurst, Dorothea E: *Horsham: Its History and Antiquities*, 1865 and 1889.

Kaye-Smith, Sheila: *Weald of Kent and Sussex*, 1953.

Kensett, WH: *Memories of Slaugham*, 1929

Latham, Charlotte: *Some West Sussex Superstitions Lingering in 1868*, 1878.

Lovett, Edward: *Folk-lore and Legends of the Surrey Hills and of the Sussex Downs and Forests*, 1928.

Lower, Mark Anthony: *Contributions to Literature*, 1854.

Lowerson, John and Myerscough, John: *Time to Spare in Victorian England*, 1977.

Lucey, Beryl: *Twenty Centuries in Sedlescombe*, 1978.

Nairn, Ian and Pevsner, Nikolaus: *The Buildings of England: Sussex*, 1965.

Parish, WD: *A Dictionary of The Sussex Dialect*, expanded edition of 1957.

Ridel, Alfred T: *Ninfield in the Nineties*, 1979.

Simpson, Jacqueline:. *The Folklore of Sussex*, 1973.

Swinfen, Warden and Arscott, David: *Hidden Sussex* series, 1980s.

Taylor, Rupert: *The East Sussex Village Book*, 1986.

Thirkell, Angela: *Three Houses*, 1931.

West Sussex Federation WIs: *West Sussex Within Living Memory*, 1993.

Wills, Barclay: *Shepherds of Sussex*, 1938.

Wolseley, Viscountess: *The Countryman's Log Book*, 1921.

Woodford, Cecile: *Portrait of Sussex*, 1975.

 By the Crown Divided, 1983.

Woodman, TC: *The South Downs*, 1901.

Wyatt, HRP: *Fragments of Findon*, 1926.

Wymer, Norman: *Companion into Sussex*, 1972.

Young, Gerard: *Cottage in the Fields*, 1945.

I have also consulted Sussex newspapers, local guides and journals, copies of *The Sussex Family Historian, Sussex Archaeological Society Collections*, and *Petworth Society Magazine*.

In particular I am deeply grateful to the contributors to the late lamented *Sussex County Magazine*, whose material never ceases to enthrall me.

ACKNOWLEDGEMENTS

I AM deeply in the debt of the many Sussex folk who have shared their memories with me. Many of them I cannot name,as I met them only briefly during talks to clubs and organisations. The following people (some sadly no longer with us) deserve my particular thanks for the help and encouragement given to me so freely.

George Attrill, Bel Bailey, F Barton, Gordon Brookes, Mabs Bryant, Lillian Candlin, Clara Chandler, RH Charters, Winifred Cousins, Cecil Cramp, Mrs Fyfield, H Goatcher, Rex Godliman, Doris Hall, Gordon Hall, Chris Hare, Richard Holmwood, Tom Holt, PH Laker, Peter Langford, Don Lewry, Bill Lindfield, Mrs Loomes, SL Longhurst, WM Loxton, Sam McCarthy-Fox, Violet Mercer, Mrs M Moiran, Harry Mousdell, Bill Muddle, Sid Neve, Mr Newnham, Cyril Phillips, Ethel Powell, Mrs S Rouse, John Sams, Scan Tester, The Rev T Tyler, Elsie Vincent, Minnie Wales, Celia Wales, Faith Woods.

For illustrations I am indebted to Stephen Granger for modern photographs; also Barbara Banks, Chichester Reference Library, CW Cramp, TJ Laker, Ralph Merrifield and R Money.

I have talked to so many good people over the many years I have been collecting folklore and folk songs, that I fear I must have omitted several who should be included, If you are one of these, then please forgive me.

ABOUT THE AUTHOR

 TONY Wales was born in Horsham in 1924 and has lived there for most of his life. Originally he worked in the music business, becoming Press and Publications Officer of the English Folk Dance and Song Society at its national headquarters, Cecil Sharp House, in London. After nearly twenty years, during which time he compiled many books on folk music, he moved on to become the London manager of the American Library of Congress.

After retirement Tony ran his own academic book-selling business for several years. For some twenty-five years he has also been writing books on Sussex folklore and old country life.

Tony Wales's previous titles are:

We Wunt be Druv, 1976
A Sussex Garland, 1979
A Day Out in Old Sussex, 1982
Long Summer Days, 1983
The West Sussex Village Book, 1984, revised 1999
Ballads, Bands and Bellringers, 1985
Horsham in Old Picture Postcards
Vol 1, 1987, *Vol 2*, 1992
An Album of Old Horsham, 1989
Sussex Customs, Curiosities and Country Lore, 1990
Sussex Ghosts and Legends, 1992
Littlehampton in Old Picture Postcards, 1993
Horsham and District in Old Photographs, 1994
Landscapes of West Sussex, 1994
Photo Archive Series: Brighton and Hove, 1997;
Bognor Regis, 1997; *Hastings*, 1998
Horsham Then and Now, 2000
Sussex as She Wus Spoke, 2000